Quit Freaking Out!

How to Stop Letting Fear and Insecurity Hold You Back

HEATHER WOCHNICK

ISBN: 1505303478
ISBN 13: 9781505303476

CONTENTS

ACKNOWLEDGMENTS

I'd like to thank my amazing husband, Mark, my son, Caleb, and my wonderful friends who encouraged me to write this book. They helped me believe in this project when I couldn't believe on my own. I especially thank God, who has taught me over and over to never let fear win.

PREFACE

Fear. Every one of us has experienced it at one time or another. We're all familiar with those heart-pounding, mind-racing, sweaty-palm moments that grip us in the face of some impending danger. Or perhaps it's that stomach-knotting sense of dread we feel when faced with a monumental task we worry that we'll be unable to accomplish.

According to *Merriam-Webster's Unabridged Dictionary*, fear is defined as "an unpleasant, often strong emotion caused by expectation or awareness of danger; anxious concern." Remember the last time a car pulled in front of you when you were going 70 mph and you had to slam on the brakes to avoid a collision? Or the moment your three-year-old dashed into the street to chase a ball as an oncoming car approached? That strong emotion of fear mobilizes us as our adrenaline soars, causing our heart to beat faster and our breathing to increase to get ready to *do* something. Fight or flight.

A small percentage of folks exist who thrive on the feeling of danger. They feel relatively little fear in life and actually create adrenaline-rushing experiences just for the thrill of it. The faster, the higher, the more dangerous, the better. A former coworker of mine had a daughter who had no fear and, as a toddler, would regularly climb out of her crib at night and begin to scale kitchen cupboards. One day, she was found dangling from a light fixture over a stairwell! Her parents were so concerned for her safety that they would sleep by her bedroom door at night to prevent her from participating in her toddler nocturnal adventures. For most of us, common sense and a less-accommodating attitude toward fear compel us to avoid danger. And frankly, that's a good thing! Fear can serve a very useful purpose. It's what prevents us from sticking our hands into fire or walking too close to a steep, rocky precipice.

Our family was driving through Yellowstone Park one year and happened to see a mama bear trailed by three bear cubs. It was a Kodak moment, and I'm happy to say we were able to capture it on film (yes, I'm dating myself). Due to a healthy fear of mother bears with their cubs, we opted to take the picture from within the confines of our vehicle. However, there were some fellow tourists who did not share our perspective and decided to get out of their vehicles to get a closeup shot. Lucky for them, they didn't end up as bear lunch. A good dose of healthy fear would have done those folks some good.

When fear turns unhealthy, it can cause us to live in a prison that keeps us from accomplishing anything from everyday tasks to major life dreams and goals. Sometimes it's packaged as insecurity, worry, doubt, and anxiety. Molehills become mountains. Fear and anxiety can create scenarios in our minds that don't exist and, in many cases, never will. Fear makes up imaginary bad endings. Have you ever experienced a time where you worried about something for days, only to have nothing happen? My pastor often uses this acronym for fear: False Evidence Appearing Real. Of course, there are times where fears can be rational, but we are so debilitated by them that we can't use the fear to propel us forward to appropriate action. Insecurity and doubt can literally stop us dead in our tracks, causing us to feel helpless and trapped.

In my work as both a professional therapist and pastor, I've worked with countless individuals with tremendous gifts, strengths, and abilities who consistently struggle with fear and insecurity, which has robbed them of the joy and fulfillment they might otherwise experience in life.

God, the giver of life and emotion, has a lot to say about fear and anxiety, especially those fears that would cripple us or trap us in an emotional and psychological prison. He never wants his children to live in bondage to fear. He wants us to live in freedom, unfettered from fear, doubt, and anxiety so that we can reach our full potential in every area of our lives.

In the pages of this book, we're going to look at God's plan and strategy for setting you free from the fears that are holding you back. It is my deepest desire that, as you read, you will find words of life and truth that will help you break off the shackles of fear in your life. Words that will release you from anxiety and doubt and help you live a life of hope and unlimited potential that faith, truth, and the grace of God produce.

The following chapters are not so much a step-by-step approach to overcoming fear as a collection of stories of people just like you and me who overcame fear, doubt, and insecurity. They are stories of the human condition and a God who loves us and takes us on a journey of freedom. Free to realize and believe in our God-given potential and significance. Free to live in a faith that moves mountains. May this book inspire and assist you as you learn to leave fear behind.

1

YOUR LIFE MATTERS

There are many circumstances in life that we don't get to choose. We don't decide who our families will be, what cities or countries we'll live in (at least in childhood), the state of the economy, or what type of temperaments we will have. People decide for us what our names will be, where we will go to school, and what laws we must live by. Lots of things are beyond our control. Now if you grew up in a loving family in a nice suburban neighborhood and attended a great school where you were popular and excelled, the fact that you didn't choose those things probably doesn't matter. However, if you're like most people, life hasn't been perfect. In fact, there might have been many things in your life that were out of your control that you wish you could have changed.

What do we do when the uncontrollables in life add up to pain and disappointment? What happens when life is unfair or even cruel? We've been physically or sexually abused, we get cancer, we lose our jobs. Perhaps a parent is an alcoholic or a brother is killed in a car accident.

Is life just a bunch of random events, and we're subject to all the forces around us, like trillions of little atoms bouncing around the universe? Is life a big lottery that some people win and others lose? Or is there some higher plan or purpose in life that brings meaning to all that seems beyond our control?

Yes, there is a higher purpose, and life is not entirely random. It's just that some days, that purpose doesn't look so obvious. But it's there, waiting to be discovered by each one of us.

Where's Your Focus?

Not long ago, I read that whatever you focus on gets magnified. Let's say you want to buy a new car (if you've got a bunch of kids, that'll probably look a lot like a minivan). You've found the exact minivan you've been looking for, with built-in child-safety seats, refrigerator, minitheater (for a minivan, of course), and seats that double as flotation devices. So you finally sign on the dotted line and drive off the car lot with your brand-new, sparkling van. As you pull up to the next stop light, there it is. The same van. You pull in to the grocery store parking lot, there's your van again. In several different colors. You see your vehicle everywhere. Why? Because it's been your focus.

If we focus on all the flaws in other people, it won't take long until it will be difficult to think of anything good about them. Soon we will be critical of everything they do. Likewise, if we focus on their positive traits, we will tend to be more tolerant and forgiving of their shortcomings and flaws.

John D. Rockefeller built the Standard Oil empire. One day, one of his executives made an error that cost the company $2 million. Of course, everyone who knew about the mistake waited for the inevitable blowup. As another of Rockefeller's executives went to meet with his boss, he found Rockefeller writing something on a piece of paper.

Rockefeller looked up and said, "I guess you've heard about the two-million-dollar mistake our friend made."

"Yes," the executive said, expecting Rockefeller to explode.

"Well, I've been sitting here listing all of our friend's good qualities on this sheet of paper, and I've discovered that in the past he has made us many more times the amount he lost for us today by his one mistake. His good points far outweigh this one human error. So I think we ought to forgive him, don't you?"[1]

What we focus on matters. So what does that have to do with there being a plan or purpose to life? If you believe life is random or totally out of your control, you won't look for purpose. A couple of things happen when someone decides to discover his life purpose. First, he begins to realize that he is significant. A life with meaning and purpose is a life of significance. Second, he discovers that more things are in his control than he originally thought. He recognizes that he has the power to choose, to make decisions, and to behave in ways that create circumstances he desires. He can, by choice, cultivate a life of meaning and purpose, even when life has been difficult.

In his book *If You Want to Walk on Water, You've Got to Get Out of the Boat*, John Ortberg cites studies that illustrate the difference between prisoners of war and hostages who maintain a sense of control in their difficult circumstances compared to those who don't. He writes:

A major theme that characterizes resilient persons is their surprising exercise of control in a stress-filled environment. Many POWs and hostages report that the single most stressful aspect of their ordeal was the realization that they had lost command over their existence. Those who lapsed into a state of passive acceptance…were the least likely to survive and recover. Amazingly enough, losing control over their daily lives was more critical to their psychological well-being than their more obvious sufferings—threats, hunger, beatings, and isolation…POWs and hostages who triumphed over adversity share a common trait—they managed to reassert a sense of command over their future. Instead of becoming passive, they focused as much attention as possible on whatever possibilities for control remained.

[Vietnam POWs] would place themselves on strenuous exercise regimens, memorize stories, or invent new games. Some ordered their time by keeping a careful census of insects in their cell. They ingeniously defied their captives' orders not to communicate with each other. Some of them developed secret signals such as taps on the wall that stood for letters of the alphabet. One prisoner used strokes of his broom to send messages in code...the POWs encouraged each other and reminded themselves that their bodies had been captured but their spirits had not.[2]

The One Who Gives Us Purpose

One of the great truths of the Bible is the fact that there is a God who created us and designed us for a specific purpose, and he desires that each of us look to him to discover it. If you weren't sure what the purpose was for a particular tool or device, you would read the manufacturer's description and instructions about it. God made you. And he didn't just throw a bunch of parts together. You have been very carefully and meticulously designed. He had a masterpiece in mind as he created you. Ephesians calls us God's workmanship:

"For we are God's workmanship, created in Christ Jesus to do good works, which God prepared in advance for us to do" (Eph. 2:10).

No matter how difficult or broken our lives have been, God longs to take all the pieces, good or bad, and create a masterpiece: a life of purpose and significance. Does that mean it was God's will that the bad, painful things happened? No. What it does mean is that he is able to work in us in such a way that regardless of what we've been through and what pain and damage it may have caused, he can heal, restore, and redeem good out of our lives. God is not only a creator; he is also a repairer. He can fix what gets broken.

You Are Not Invisible to God

There's a story in the Bible about a woman named Hagar. Speaking of crummy, out-of-her-control circumstances, Hagar was a maidservant. Not exactly a dream job. She lived in a culture in which women were treated more like property than human beings. Her master was a man named Abraham, who had been given a promise from God that he would be the father of a great nation, Israel. Not only would Israel be powerful and influential, but it would also produce the Messiah, the savior of the world, Jesus Christ.

Because of Abraham's faith and trust in God, God had a big, supernatural plan for his life. Supernatural because Sarah, his wife, was barren. Not only that, but they were both getting up there in years. We're talking *retirement* years. Instead of going on cruises and playing golf, they were going to be changing diapers and up for midnight feedings! At first, the idea seemed so absurd that they laughed. Eventually, they decided they would trust God and wait for the miracle (see Gen. 18:11–15). Like most of us, they got tired of waiting. So they took matters into their own hands and decided to use a surrogate, their maidservant Hagar. And we all know that when we take matters into *our* hands that God is supposed to have in *his* hands, we usually mess things up (see Gen. 16:1–15). Hagar gets pregnant and the fireworks begin! Sarah becomes resentful and makes life miserable for Hagar. Hagar, in turn, despises and mistreats Sarah. Was Hagar's situation fair? Did she choose it? Nope.

Perhaps you were forced into a situation that wasn't your idea, like your parents got a divorce or your dad got a new job out of state and you had to move away from a place you loved. Maybe you responded negatively, and as a result, the situation got worse.

I've done it. Growing up, I experienced some hard circumstances beyond my control. Some of my responses to those circumstances were destructive, and the consequences began to play out. I hurt others and others hurt me. Hagar and Sarah began to hurt each other. When Hagar could no longer stand Sarah's treatment, she ran away from her mistress and found herself all alone in a desert by a spring, headed toward a wilderness.

Sometimes that's where difficult circumstances can feel like they lead us: into a desert or wilderness. Not a literal wilderness, but an emotional wilderness. We run to things like alcohol, unhealthy relationships, workaholism, or an affair, anything that looks like an escape. Hagar impulsively ran from her situation, only to find that running doesn't solve anything. Except now she was alone and pregnant, with nowhere to go.

As Hagar was sitting by a spring in the desert, the Angel of the Lord appeared to her. This was none other than God himself. He began by asking Hagar where she had come from and where she was going. Now if this was really God speaking, didn't he already know the answer? Of course, but the question grabbed Hagar's attention and caused her to do a little personal inventory. Sometimes a question like that is exactly what we need when we've headed into a wilderness and lost our way. A question that makes us stop and think is, "How did I get here?" Hagar couldn't fully answer the question. She had no idea where she was going, only where she came from.

Hagar responded, "I'm running away from my mistress, Sarah." First, God told her to put her life back into its proper order, "return to your mistress and submit to her authority."

Perhaps it seemed odd for the Lord to tell her to return to a situation that was difficult and painful. Here's where we discover the wisdom of God. He taught Hagar that she must be responsible for her actions, regardless of what has been done to her. He also taught her that running away doesn't solve things. God didn't just tell her to go back; he gave her encouragement about her future. He told her about the child she was carrying, his destiny, and the descendants that would come from his line. God had plans and purposes for Hagar and the child she was carrying. God sees a future we're often blind to, especially when we're in the midst of dismal situations.

Here, we discover a profound truth that is the foundation, the beginning, of the journey from fear to faith. God sees Hagar and reaches out to her. A God she wasn't even personally serving. A God who showed up in the midst of her biggest failure and scariest place and told her he was listening, "for the Lord has heard your cry of distress." From that point on, her discovery of God causes her to address him in a new way. She called him El-Roi, "You are the God who sees me."

The journey begins when we discover that we are not alone and life is not totally random and out of our control. In the midst of the wilderness, the lonely place without answers or hope, there is a God who sees and listens to us. There is no place too remote, no circumstance too dark, no hole too deep that God can't find us. He doesn't just see us; he gives us a way out, a hope, and a future.

Before you can believe and trust in a God you don't know, you have to discover that he really exists. He sees you right where you are and he hears you. He is not an absent, distant cosmic force. He's a personal God. He wants to show up in your life. He wants to show up in the messiest parts of your life, *even if you created the mess.* He loves you and cares. Slowly, the fear of not knowing where to go and what to do is addressed by God's wisdom— "return to what is right." This *is* in your control to do.

I can relate to Hagar. Because of painful life circumstances, in frustration and desperation I left the path that was right. I ran to a wilderness of alcohol and drugs. I was scared and alone with nowhere to turn, until one day an angel showed up in my life. Her name was Melody. Not a real angel, but I believe she was sent by God. She began to share God's love with me when I was at the end of my rope. That day, God let me know that he saw me; he was my El Roi. He found me in my wilderness. I cried out to him and he heard me. He not only got me back on the right track, but, like Hagar, he had much better plans for my future. That was the beginning of my journey from fear to faith.

Journey Out of the Darkest Fear—Mary's Story

Mary (not her real name) grew up in a home that you wouldn't wish on your worst enemy. Her parents were in a traveling band and took Mary on the road with them. By the time Mary was three years old, her parents' marriage had fallen apart, and they soon divorced. Her mother was declared unfit, and her father was given custody. Mary's father continued on his road tour and decided Mary should live with his mother, a strong Christian woman, hoping that life in a home without travel would give Mary some stability. Mary loved her grandmother and her grandmother loved her dearly. It was the best time of Mary's young life. By the time Mary turned six, her father had remarried and decided that Mary should live with him and his new wife. Mary was excited at the possibility of having a "mom" and decided to give her a chance. Mary tried to love her new stepmom, but her stepmom didn't love her back. In fact, Mary would soon discover that she was an angry, domineering woman who would assume control of her father, his band, and Mary in ways that were unimaginably horrible. Filled with anger and resentment, Mary and her father became the targets of her rage and hatred. First came the abusive words, hair-pulling, and slapping. Then came the isolation. Mary would be left alone, sometimes for days on end. Mary's father was very passive and let his new wife do whatever she wanted without protecting Mary. He would often disappear for days at a time.

Mary's stepmother had wanted to conceive but wasn't able to. This only fueled her resentment toward Mary, and the first of many beatings began. When Mary was nine, her parents stayed permanently in a dumpy motel, leaving Mary by herself with the family dog in their RV, which they parked across the highway. The only food Mary had was a jug filled with water, a loaf of bread, and some peanut butter to last for the week. Mary was often starving and would eat the dog's food in order to survive.

Mary, in her own words:

For days at a time I was left in my room. My stepmom would put Scotch tape over the door so that the tape would break if I opened it. She would beat me badly if I broke the tape. Dad would be gone for days at a time doing his work. She would punish him by giving him a whole list of things I had done wrong (which were lies). First order of business was dealing with the list, and she would have dad beat me. He would have to take my pants down and whip me thirty, forty, or fifty times with a belt, depending on how long her list was. I would have to hold on to the wall or ladder during the beatings, and if I took my hands off, he would have to start over. If my dad didn't hit me hard enough, she would stop counting until he hit me harder. I began hardening my heart toward her and began to hate her. When I was thirteen or fourteen years old, I was washing dishes one day. I had a butcher knife in the water. She came in, grabbed me by the hair, and wielded a frying pan in her hands like she was going to hit me. I remember thinking I was going to put the knife through the middle of her chest. She walked out of the kitchen. I didn't know if I was disappointed that I wanted to kill her or that I didn't do it.

I would go three or four days without food. My parents would lock me up for days with no food and then make me clean the house. I would lie in bed and cry at night. I missed my grandmother, and I loved my mom. Mom would care for me differently than Dad, but she had a gambling addiction. On my one week per year with my mom, she would buy me a Happy Meal and some magazines, and then she would go to a casino, leaving me locked in the car. I thought she was great because she fed me and didn't beat me. I wanted to be with her so much. I would pray that someday I would get rescued. I told God if he would get me out of there, I would give him my life. One day, my stepmom flew to Hawaii. My dad was at home and scared but let me out of my room. Twenty-four hours later, he handed me a paper bag, told me to pack my things, and said I was leaving. My mom's parents showed up and rushed me into a car, and we drove away. I was fourteen. My dad told me good-bye, and I didn't see him again for seven years.

All sympathy for my dad began to dissolve. I stopped feeling sorry for him and began to realize that he was an adult. I had watched my dad get beaten by his wife, but I realized he had the power to change it for both of us and didn't. When that became clear, I hated him. I forgot about God. I entered into what I call "the great numbness." Instead of going to bed at night crying with compassion for my dog, my dad, and my mom, I began going to bed at night rehearsing a great drama I was scripting to kill my dad and stepmom. Every night, I pictured tracking them down and putting a gun to their heads. I had nightmares every single night after getting away from them that they were chasing me and bringing me back. I would dream the same dream seven or eight times a night.

I began living with my stepdad (my biological mom had re-married). Right before I turned seventeen, my stepdad said I had to get out of his house. I packed a backpack and left. I moved in with a friend, and when she turned eighteen, we got an apartment. I needed more money so I "auditioned" at a hole-in-the-wall topless bar. I was making $200–$250 a night. After I turned eighteen, I went to a metropolitan area to work at a big club and went into full-blown stripping. My first night I made over a thousand dollars. Although I never used hard drugs, I mixed Valium with vodka so I could sleep at night.

I was also deep into astrology. I didn't make a single decision unless the planets and stars aligned. I would hang out in the mystical section of bookstores. One day I bought a book called *The Late Great Planet Earth* by Hal Lindsey. It had been accidently placed in the mystical section, and I thought the title was interesting. I had no idea it was a book on the Bible's teaching on the end times! While I was reading the book, all of a sudden I began hating my life. I didn't associate it with the book; I just was coming to the end of myself. I had run so far from God, I think I accidently ran into him with that book!

I continued to read Hal Lindsey. My dreams began getting worse. Then, out of nowhere, I had a night where I just felt pain inside my heart. I had been numb for so long that when I felt it, I thought it would kill me. I was alone in my apartment and tried to make my way to the kitchen, but the pain in my heart literally pulled me to my knees. I bowed down and began praying to God. I don't remember what I said, but I think it was "help me." I stayed on the floor for a while and felt like something was so different that night. I went into my bedroom with all my astrology books, and there was my Hal Lindsay book and a Bible. I had no recollection as to where that Bible came from. I opened it and it had my name written in it in my own seven-year-old handwriting. I had nothing from when I was a little girl. When I left my house I had only a paper bag with a few belongings. I don't have any idea where this Bible came from.

I sat down and began to read the New Testament. I began with one of the gospels and read all the way through. I got to the place where Jesus was praying in the garden of Gethsemane for everyone who was going to come to know him. I had a vision of Jesus kneeling at a big rock praying the words I had been reading. In my mind, Jesus looked straight into my eyes and said, "This is for you." Then he began to explain to me that what he was praying about was for me. I thought I had imagined it and was totally crazy. The emotional pain came flooding back. All at once, I realized I was a sinner. It was in that moment, I became alive and began to feel everything I couldn't feel all those years. I began to cry again, not because I was a stripper, but because I was a sinner and had run from God. I cried because I had murder in my heart. I told God I would live for him if he rescued me. I knew Jesus was on the floor there with me. I begged him not to let me feel this, but I knew he was opening a door for me to be set free. But he made it clear to me that before I could get off the floor and move forward with him, I had to forgive my dad. I wrestled a long time with it. I was afraid to let it go. I would have to lay down the only power I ever felt I had. I don't remember the exact words I prayed, but I agreed with Jesus I would not take anyone's life. Not my dad or my stepmom. I laid the vengeance down. In exchange I wanted him to take the pain I was feeling and fix me. That night, for the first time in six years, I had no dreams or nightmares. No Valium or vodka. No numbness or fantasies of killing anyone. I went to bed and got up the next day alive. I went into the bathroom and looked in the mirror. I stared at my face. I looked like a different person! I knew Jesus had been there. I woke up with faith. There was no church, no altar call. I had just encountered Christ."

Today, Mary's life is radically different. She is married to a godly, Christian man, and they have four children, one who has a calling to be a pastor and another who wants to become a missionary. The Lord has created a masterpiece in Mary. Her life has significance and purpose that only the God of the universe could create, even out of the most horrific circumstances.

The journey from fear to faith always begins with an encounter with the God who sees us, the God who knows right where we are and loves us. He is waiting to hear us cry out to him. He listens and cares.

What is causing you fear right now? Is there turmoil in your life? Do you feel like you're in a wilderness? God sees you right where you are, and he hears the cry of your heart. Listen to his quiet voice whispering to you...Is he asking you a question? Is he giving you a gentle instruction or a promise for your future? Or is he just assuring you that he is there?

Let this truth start you on a new journey of faith. Your God sees you, and he's listening.

2

SCARED TO DEATH

Probably most of us at one time or another have heard someone say, "I was scared to death!" or "You scared me to death!" Most likely we heard it from our well-meaning mothers when we did something that freaked them out, like forgetting to tell them we were going to play at the neighbor's house when we were five years old or practicing our Spiderman moves by jumping from a tree branch onto the roof of the house.

Have you ever wondered if it's really possible to be scared to death? According to a 2009 article in *Scientific American*, it is indeed. The article tells the story of a man in Charlotte, North Carolina, who was charged with the first-degree murder of a seventy-nine-year-old woman. Police said she died when the man broke into her home to hide after botching a bank robbery. The man had not touched her, but she suffered a fatal heart attack that was triggered by the terror she felt.[1]

A 2012 article from *The Wall Street Journal* states that doctors around the world are seeing unusual heart problems in people who are normally healthy but have experienced severe fright, trauma, or loss of a loved one. [2] It comes in the form of sudden heart failure, known as stress cardiomyopathy.

One doctor described nineteen cases of stress cardiomyopathy in the *New England Journal of Medicine* in 2005, and since that time, thousands of patients around the world have been diagnosed with the condition.

On January 17, 1994, there was an earthquake in the Los Angeles area in which over one hundred Californians died of fear, according to a cardiologist at the Good Samaritan Hospital in Los Angeles.

The chairman of the neurology department at Brigham and Women's Hospital in Boston, Dr. Martin A. Samuels, has gathered hundreds of reports of people dying suddenly as a result of being severely frightened. According to his reports, the events causing death varied greatly, from children dying on amusement park rides, to victims of muggings and break-ins who were never touched, and victims in car crashes who sustained only minor injuries. One man died from heart damage as he jumped from the roof of the hospital. Dr. Samuels also tells a story of his cat's encounter with a field mouse. His cat held the mouse by the tail, batted it around, and within twenty minutes, the mouse died in spite of the fact that it suffered no significant injuries. According to Samuels, animals experience this same phenomenon that humans do.

So what causes this "scared to death" phenomenon? It has to do with the protective system we were wired with, called the "flight or fight" response. When we are in perceived danger, our brain responds by activating the sympathetic nervous system, which sends a surge of adrenaline and other chemicals to various parts of the body. These chemicals increase a person's heart rate and blood pressure, causing more blood to flow to the muscles to prepare the body for action. However, the chemical adrenaline is toxic to the body in large amounts and can cause damage to organs such as the heart, liver, kidneys, and lungs. In most cases, it is the heart that cannot sustain the damage and quickly fails, producing death.

Fortunately, it is only a small percentage of people who actually die of fear. That's the good news! The bad news is that fear and anxiety, even if they don't kill us, certainly can do their share of damage to our bodies in the form of stress-related illnesses like high blood pressure, heart disease, diabetes, and obesity. Not to mention the emotional toll regular fear and anxiety take on us.

While life certainly gives us many opportunities to face fearful situations, we human beings seem prone to take fear to many irrational levels. Ever heard of ephebiphobia? It's a fear and loathing of youth or teenagers. Not teen gang members. Just teens in general. I realize for some of you parents of teenagers, you may be wondering why the fear is irrational! However, for the record, it is considered a pathological fear. Ergasiophobia or ergophobia is an intense fear of finding work or being employed. There is the fear of feathers, called pteronophobia. There is taphophobia, the fear of being buried alive. And last but certainly not least, a phobia that I personally deal with, nochocolaphobia, the fear of running out of chocolate. OK, I made that one up, but I do have that fear.

Many of us battle fear of the future, fear of being of rejected, fear of failure, even fear of success. The list is endless. The bottom line is, we human beings battle much fear and anxiety in life, and not all of it is irrational. There are things that we should legitimately fear, because they are in fact harmful to us in some way.

So how are we supposed to deal with all the fears and anxieties that afflict us? God has much to say on the matter of fear and anxiety in the Bible. I've heard that the Bible has 365 occurrences of God telling us not to be afraid. While I'm not certain that number is accurate, I do know for a fact that there are many biblical references of God telling his people "fear not." Or do not be anxious. Enough times to make the point that God doesn't want us living in fear and anxiety. Many of the references are in the context of God being our helper in hard situations so that we don't need to fear. The Bible says that we should cast all our cares and anxieties on God because he cares for us.

"Cast your cares on the LORD and he will sustain you" (Ps. 55:22).

"Cast all your anxiety on him because he cares for you" (1 Pet. 5:7).

God encourages us to *not* be anxious at all, but instead to ask for his help in all situations, thank him in faith for what he will do, and when we do that, he will respond by giving us peace.

"Do not be anxious about anything, but in everything, by prayer and petition, with thanksgiving, present your requests to God. And the peace of God, which transcends all understanding, will guard your hearts and your minds in Christ Jesus" (Phil. 4:6–7).

When Jesus said he'd give us life more abundantly, I believe he meant in the area of our emotions, too. One of the many benefits of having a personal relationship with Christ is that it includes a peace that the world can't give us. We have a source much bigger and more powerful than ourselves to help us, strengthen us, and care for our needs. We don't have to go it alone. Peace in this life can be hard to come by, but it is a promise from God.

In chapter 11, I'll explore the idea that when we have a reverent respect or "fear" of God, it is meant to dispel almost all other fear. Literally, the fear of God replaces all other irrational fear, because of the supernatural peace God wants us to live in. It's not always easy to get to that total "peace zone," but God gives us a lot of instructions in the Bible to help us get there.

Much of what causes us fear in life is based on lies or irrational thinking. Anxiety creates mountains out of molehills. Many of us live in fear that we have created in our minds. In the next few chapters, I'll address many of the false beliefs that keep people bound in fear, anxiety, and insecurity.

One of the many powerful descriptions of Jesus Christ is that he is the truth. He's not described as having truth, or knowing truth; He is called *the* truth. All that is true, all that is honest, all that is trustworthy and accurate is found in Jesus Christ.

Jesus taught that when we really understood his truth, it would set us free. He wants to break all the flawed, fallacious, distorted, and inaccurate beliefs that hold us captive to fear and anxiety. The heartbeat of God is that we, as his creation, would know that we can live in love, forgiveness, and freedom from fear and condemnation. One of the biggest ploys of our spiritual enemy, Satan, is to lie to us. He wants us to believe that God doesn't exist, or he doesn't love us, or that he isn't really who he says he is.

Satan is the accuser and condemner. He is relentless in his attempts to make us feel as though we've failed, God is not happy with us, and that we are not good enough. He screams at us about our unworthiness and weakness and tries to get us to believe that God doesn't really love us. That God will not work on our behalf because we don't measure up. Satan is called the Father of Lies for a reason. He uses deception ruthlessly. It is my hope and prayer that within the pages of this book are truths that will dismantle the lies Satan has used to hold so many good people captive. And that these truths will build faith and confidence in the God who has ordained so many precious promises, hopes, and dreams for his children.

In the next chapter, we begin with the truth about a force so vast and so powerful that it is the very foundation of freedom from fear. Every other truth builds on it.

It is revolutionary. It is transformative. It is love.

3

A LOVE GREATER THAN FEAR

As a young teenage girl, fear and insecurity caused me escape into a world of alcohol and drugs. My fourteenth birthday was the beginning of many drinking binges. I began doing things that endangered my life and damaged relationships. Soon, drugs followed. After I'd heard several critical comments about my weight, I began starving myself and developed an eating disorder. I loathed myself and at times had thoughts of suicide. When I was eighteen, a good friend of mine visited me at college. We had partied together many times in high school. He had recently committed his life to Jesus Christ, and I could see immediately that something was different about him. I could see joy and peace on his face that I'd never seen before. He introduced me to his brother, a strong Christian, who lived on campus. His brother led a Bible study that I began to attend where I met other students who were devout in their Christian faith. I saw the same joy in them that I saw in my friend. They never judged me or criticized how I acted. For the first time in my life, I experienced the unconditional love of God through these new friends.

Later that year, I committed my life to Christ. I truly wanted to leave my old life behind and receive the life Christ had for me. I felt overwhelmed with the love and forgiveness of Jesus, and my journey of emotional healing began as Christ showed me what unconditional love and acceptance was.

You see, I had lived so many years feeling like I wasn't good enough. I wasn't smart enough, pretty enough, obedient enough, emotionally strong enough, or athletic enough. Striving to be better was a constant compulsion. Striving to please my parents. Striving to be accepted at school. Striving to be pretty or skinny enough. It felt like a never-ending battle, and I was always on the losing side. I was always trying to earn people's approval and acceptance. When I encountered the love of Christ, it was the first time I ever felt accepted without having to strive for it. I was loved just as I was, no strings or striving attached. I was forgiven without having to earn it. I didn't have to figure out how to be good enough. The grace of God that was extended to me was a free gift. It's a promise God gives all of us in Ephesians 2:8–9 (NLT): "God saved you by his grace when you believed. And you can't take credit for this; it is a gift from God. Salvation is not a reward for the good things we have done, so none of us can boast about it."

When I received Christ's love and forgiveness, I felt like I got a brand-new start in life. It was the beginning of what God had designed and intended for my life. The next verse in Ephesians 2 states it like this:

"For we are God's masterpiece. He has created us anew in Christ Jesus, so we can do the good things he planned for us long ago" (Eph. 2:10 NLT).

God had created me, and the enemy and sin tried to destroy my life. But because of God's incredible, unconditional love, he extended grace and forgiveness freely to me when I chose to put my faith in him. My life is meant to be a masterpiece, with good things flowing from it. That has always been God's design for not only my life, but yours, too. Your life is a masterpiece. Perhaps you haven't taken the step yet to allow God to create you anew, to give you a fresh start, but he loves you as you are and anxiously longs to give you the abundant life he has planned for you. And it's never too late. It's a free gift for you. You don't have to earn it; you just have to receive it in faith.

After I initially committed my life to Christ, I began a lifelong journey of learning what it is to be a follower of Christ. Many old, destructive patterns of thinking had to change to align to the truths God had for me. In chapter 8, I'll talk about something I call a mental stronghold, a deeply held, false belief that has a destructive grip on our lives. I've had to break many of those.

Grace Pardons Failure

About five years into my Christian journey, one of those strongholds reared its ugly head. I began experiencing an incredible sense of condemnation regarding my relationship with God. The fear of not measuring up gripped me as I wrestled with the sense that I wasn't reading my Bible, praying, or sharing my faith enough. Of course there are times where most of us could apply ourselves a little more diligently in those areas, but this was a debilitating fear of God's punishment. I was certain he was very displeased with me. I still loved Jesus and wanted to live for him, but I felt like no matter how hard I tried, I would never be good enough.

Just as I was ready to throw in the towel, God's still, small voice said, "Heather, what were you when I saved you?"

I answered, "A mess." God saved me when my life was at its *worst*! I did nothing to deserve it. I wasn't saved because I was good enough; I was saved and would remain saved *by his gift of grace alone*. Romans 3:23–24 says that we've all fallen short of God's standard and are incapable of living up to it on our own, but he gives us his generous gift of grace:

"Since we've compiled this long and sorry record as sinners (both us and them) and proved that we are utterly incapable of living the glorious lives God wills for us, God did it for us. Out of sheer generosity he put us in right standing with himself. A pure gift. He got us out of the mess we're in and restored us to where he always wanted us to be. And he did it by means of Jesus Christ" (Rom. 3:23–24 MSG).

The love and grace of God I had once known became cloudy because of perfectionistic fear. In chapter 5, I'll address the lie of perfectionism in greater depth. As God lovingly reminded me again of his grace, peace flooded my mind and emotions. One of the most beautiful, profound messages in the Bible is the message of the grace of God that we have through faith in Christ. God's grace speaks directly to the issue of "not good enough." Grace is the supernatural enabling us to be "good enough." The grace of God pardons failure. That means we are allowed to fail. Not intentionally or willfully, but as part of the practical reality that we are all imperfect.

"Therefore, since we have been justified through faith, *we have peace with God* through our Lord Jesus Christ, through whom *we have gained access by faith into this grace in which we now stand.* And we rejoice in the hope of the glory of God" (Rom. 5:1–2, emphasis mine).

The grace of God makes us strong where we are weak. There is allowance for weakness and failure. Grace doesn't excuse sin or moral failure, but it allows us to be set free from it. Grace brings forgiveness, hope, and unlimited potential. The apostle Paul was praying about a weakness he was struggling with—in fact the Bible says he begged God three times to take it away. Look at Jesus's reply:

"Each time he [Jesus] said, 'My grace is all you need. My power works best in weakness.' So now I am glad to boast about my weaknesses, so that the power of Christ can work through me" (2 Cor. 12:9–10 NLT).

Paul came to a place of peace about his weaknesses, because the grace of God caused the power of Christ to work through him in spite of his weaknesses.

The Love of God Casts Out Fear

After God spoke to me, I felt peace come over me again, and I knew things were OK between God and me. I spent many years as a Christian, though, working through that grip of fear.

One day, as I was driving my car, God the Father said, "You keep me at an arm's distance from you. You are so afraid I'm going to be displeased with you. I want to be close to you. I love you." As I heard his voice, I began to weep. I realized in that moment, I had projected on my heavenly father some of my experiences with people on earth. I wanted so much to be free of the fear I had of my heavenly father. I started on a journey of seeking God to give me a deeper revelation of his love and who he really is, not what I imagined him to be in my fears. Over the years, God has shown me very personally that he is infinitely more patient, compassionate, loving, and gracious than I had ever imagined.

As I sought to know him better, I began to see scriptures differently. They began to reveal the loving side of God more than I had ever seen before. I used to interpret certain scriptures in a way that put God in a punishing or angry light. I focused on times in the Bible where he was angry, and I believed that was his nature. However, as I pushed through my deepest fears and pursued understanding, a flood of new revelations came. Even when he was angry in the Bible, I could see his grace and compassion toward his people. His deepest desire was to get his people back on the right track. He wasn't a wrathful God. In fact, I could see that wrath wasn't his plan for his people. Correction and discipline was, but only to get them back into a healthy, right relationship with him. Only in his people's worst rebellion and wickedness did God use severe punishment, and that was after many patient, gracious responses and warnings.

Psalm 106 is a detailed account of many miraculous things God did for his people, Israel. Over and over, Israel rebelled against the Lord. Repeatedly, he would continue to work on their behalf, rescuing them, feeding them, guiding them, and protecting them. The psalmist writes that they were bent on rebellion and provoked God's anger. And yet, in spite of the many times he had previously delivered them (verse 43), he was again merciful and compassionate toward them, taking note of their cries. Out of his great love, he relented from further punishment.

"Many times he delivered them, but they were bent on rebellion and they wasted away in their sin. But he took note of their distress when he heard their cry; for their sake he remembered his covenant and *out of his great love he relented*. He caused them to be pitied by all who held them captive" (Ps. 106:43–46, emphasis mine).

For many years, I've heard the verse "perfect love drives out fear" (1 John 4:18) used as a fix for any and all fear. The thought goes something like this: "If we only knew the love of God well enough, we'd never fear anything." But as I really looked at the verse, I saw that it was referring to a specific type of fear: the fear of punishment.

"If anyone acknowledges that Jesus is the Son of God, God lives in him, and he in God. And so we know and rely on the love God has for us. God is love. Whoever lives in love lives in God, and God in him. In this way, love is made complete among us so that we will have confidence on the Day of Judgment, because in this world we are like him. There is no fear in love. But perfect love drives out fear, *because fear has to do with punishment*" (1 John 4:15–18, emphasis mine).

It says that when we know and live in the love of God, we don't fear his judgment. God's perfect, unconditional love drives out the fear we experience when we anticipate God's punishment in relationship to his judgment of us (verse 17). In other words, when we get a true understanding of how much God loves us, how unconditionally he loves us, we are truly secure in our relationship with him and no longer live in fear of punishment from him.

According to these verses, it is impossible to live in the love of God and have a fear of his judgment. Those two things should not coexist together. If we truly acknowledge Jesus Christ as our Savior, we live in God, and God *is love*.

Believe God's Word. His perfect love for you means you no longer have to fear punishment for every failure or sin. Perfect love drives out fear of *failure*.

What child with truly loving, compassionate parents runs around feeling terrified of them all the time? Sounds a little silly, doesn't it? Even if good parents need to bring correction to a misbehaving child (and they do!), correction is administered in love. The child is still secure in his or her relationship with the parents.

Rely on God's Love

1 John 4:16 says we can know and rely on the love God has for us. Something that is reliable is trustworthy, true, and dependable. Do you know what that means? We don't have to rely on ourselves to be perfect! I don't have to figure out how to be good enough, and neither do you.

Verse 17 says that reliance on God's love instead of ourselves makes us confident, because it's not about how good we are or how perfectly we are able to live the Christian life; it's about the life and love of Christ *at work in us*. Be confident. You are loved!

An Advocate When We Sin

As the Lord has continued to give me a deeper revelation of his love and grace, it has made coming to him in my times of sin much easier. Instead of wanting to hide when I fail him, I want to run *to* him and make things right, because I'm met with unconditional love and grace. He longs for you and me to be close to him, and sin can drive us apart. So he makes himself fully available to us when we want to be forgiven and right with him. When we sin, Jesus is our advocate, not our enemy (1 John 2:1–2). An advocate is one who speaks in defense of another. Jesus speaks in your defense to the Father. Not because of your righteousness, but because of his. And his love covers a multitude of sins (1 Peter 4:8). A multitude. How many times do you sin? A multitude of times? Me, too. But his love and grace has it covered. Go to him. In 1 John 1:19 we read: "If we confess our sins, He is faithful and just and will forgive us and purify us from all our unrighteousness." It's a promise. It's his love.

How often our enemy, Satan, screams an entirely different message at us. His message is always one of how bad, how broken, and how messed up we are. Satan is called the accuser, and for good reason. Even if you haven't struggled with a perfectionistic fear of failure, your adversary, the devil, is determined to make you feel like you are condemned. He wants to drive you and me away from Christ. If Satan can get us to live under constant condemnation, we will be afraid to get close to God or trust him. Fear is a device Satan uses to drive us from God. Romans 8:1 says, "Therefore, there is now no condemnation for those who are in Christ Jesus." Satan would like us to live believing the opposite is true. Condemnation can make us want to give up. It can cripple us and cause us to believe God is not for us. But that's a lie. You are free from guilt, shame, and condemnation in Christ.

As I've grown in my journey of understanding God's love and grace, it hasn't caused me to throw caution (or morality!) to the wind because he loves me unconditionally. In fact, it has done the opposite. Experiencing God's love and grace, experiencing his purity and goodness, has only caused me to desire to be more like him. He's beautiful. The Bible tells us to worship him in the beauty of his holiness. Have you ever thought about that? That the holiness of God is really beautiful because there is so much goodness to it? True holiness isn't about a bunch of outward actions; it's about a pure, good heart. It's about a heart of unconditional love and benevolence. Jesus knows we struggle with sin, but he made a way for us to be forgiven and cleansed. He made a way for our hearts to be made clean and pure so that his beauty can be seen in and through us. What an amazing promise.

All God requires is that we genuinely acknowledge our sins, turn away from them, and believe that Christ will truly forgive us and purify us. If we sin, we have an advocate (1 John 1:7–2:2). It doesn't say if we sin, we have a God who will pour out wrath on us. Or that he will reject us. Jesus advocates for us to his Father, reminding the Father that our sins are atoned for by his sacrifice. We are defended in our weakness and failure by the grace and love of Christ. Not because we deserve it or have earned it. Simply because our God longs for us to be in a relationship with him, and was willing to pay the price for our sins. God had his son take our punishment! Perfect love casts out the fear of failure. Perfect love gives us freedom to be ourselves, without fear.

In faith, believe in what Christ has done for you. You are free in Christ!

4

FAILURE IS NOT A DEAL BREAKER

Over the years, I've struggled with the fear that I would somehow mess up God's plans for my life. Most often the fear comes in the form of questioning my ability to hear him correctly and know his will. I know that is not an uncommon concern for many Christians and, perhaps in some ways, is rather normal. After all, it isn't always easy to be certain one has heard from God clearly, and it often takes years of practice and spiritual growth to become more confident in discerning the voice of God.

However, Jesus assured all of us who would follow after him that we would be able to hear him when he said, "My sheep hear my voice" (John 10:27 NKJV). There are a couple of powerful things implied in those words. One is that we *do* hear him, not just that we *will* hear him, and not just in some far-off future or in a hyperspiritual, burning-bush experience. In fact, he couldn't make the analogy much simpler than using the relationship of a shepherd and his sheep. Several years ago, I read a book by Phillip Keller titled *A Shepherd Looks at Psalm 23*. Keller was a shepherd and had a very personal understanding of the relationship a shepherd had with his sheep. He described that if several flocks of sheep with different shepherds were mixed together, they could still recognize the voice of their own shepherd and would listen to him exclusively. Sheep are not terribly complicated creatures—well, OK, the fact is, they are not very bright. Not the most flattering comparison, however, it makes a powerful point about our ability to hear God's voice. We don't have to be rocket scientists, nor do we have to have a burning-bush experience to hear from God. All that is required is a personal, interactive relationship with God. We give him our time and attention in life to build our relationship with him. We talk (pray) and he listens. He talks (through the Word, by his still, small voice, through others) and we listen. It is really meant to be as simple as a shepherd caring for his sheep. Implied in Jesus's statement that his sheep hear his voice is the fact that we can have a personal connection with God and that he *will* speak and we *do* have the ability to hear him.

Sometimes we may hear him speak, but we don't recognize it as his voice. As with learning any new skill, it takes practice and understanding, and so it is with recognizing God's voice. Often it's a matter of knowing the various ways he communicates and becoming familiar with the peace, assurance, or conviction that we feel when the message is from God.

If this is common to all Christians, then you'd think it wouldn't be a fear-producing issue. In my case, it became a problem because not hearing him correctly meant certain disaster, according to my skewed, perfectionistic thinking. It was as though if I got it wrong, somehow irreparable damage would be done, and there was no hope for God to redirect and get things back on track. My fears turned the molehill into a mountain. I call it "catastrophizing." I somehow determined, unintentionally, that God wasn't big enough to correct my misunderstanding or help me correct any mistakes that could potentially arise from an incorrect decision. Neither of those is true, but then again, fear-based beliefs are often irrational.

Paralyzed Decision Making

Holding the irrational belief that missing the mark means disaster, I would become paralyzed in decision making. Many good-hearted Christians get stuck in this fear-based decision-making process. Sometimes it subtly manifests itself as individuals' constant need to ask others for their opinion. They talk to person after person, hoping that some advice somewhere will give them the peace and assurance they are looking for. However, because fear is still motivating them, even if God does speak to them through another person, the Word of God, or directly by the Holy Spirit, their insecurity dismisses it. Either they will continue to ask more people for their advice, or they will perpetually "wait" on the Lord. Their answer will always be, "I'm still waiting on the Lord." That "waiting" is only a spiritual veneer of insecurity and "stuckness." As a result, they do nothing at all. No action produces no results, good or bad.

If God wants to do things in and through our lives, then we cannot let the fear of making a mistake paralyze us. If "getting it wrong" was a deal breaker with God, then the events in the Garden of Eden would have stopped God's plans and purposes for all human beings. The only thing that can stop God's plans for us is for us to do nothing.

"What if I forgive that person and he hurts me again?"

"What if you forgive him and you are set free from emotional pain that you've carried for years?"

"What if I reach out to her and she rejects me?"

"What if you reach out to her and your act of love is a turning point in her life?"

"What if I write the book and no one reads it?"

"What if you write the book and thousands of lives are impacted?"

The rewards of doing God's will are too great to sacrifice on the altar of fear.

Grace Happens

So what happens if we are trying to follow God and live out his purpose for our lives, but we make mistakes along the way? Grace happens. What do I mean by "grace happens"? Grace is the supernatural supply of help and power we need for every situation in our lives, whether it's power to overcome sin or power to do things God wants us to do that we think we can't do.

Grace allows us to be blameless before God, regardless of what we've done in our lives that would cause us to feel unworthy. Grace wipes the slate clean and gives us a fresh start. Grace teaches us the right way. Grace allows for our mistakes. God forgives when we mess up. His grace gives us another chance and teaches us what to do the next time.

"For the grace of God has appeared that offers salvation to all people. It teaches us to say "No" to ungodliness and worldly passions, and to live self-controlled, upright and godly lives in this present age, while we wait for the blessed hope—the appearing of the glory of our great God and Savior, Jesus Christ" (Titus 2:11-13)

Believe it or not, God wants you to be successful and prosper in what you do. Grace is what allows that to happen. In fact, Jesus said it is all you need to overcome any hindrances to his purposes for your life. Grace is the power of Christ at work in you.

Grace doesn't give us an excuse to sin or do what is wrong (see Romans 6:1–2). Grace helps us do what is right. It gives us power to do what we think we are too weak to do. The grace of God will reveal the true significance and greatest potential of your life, because you will no longer be limited by yourself. Grace can take you beyond yourself, because the power of Christ will work through you.

Grace Never Gives Up

Throughout the Bible are examples of godly people who made really big mistakes, yet God continued to work in and through their lives to accomplish the plans he had for them. In chapter 1, I shared the story of Abraham and Sarah. One of their biggest mistakes was using Hagar to try to accomplish what God wanted to do supernaturally. In spite of the unfortunate and somewhat painful consequences for everyone involved, it never stopped God from using Abraham and Sarah in the way he wanted. God's response to their failure wasn't to give up on them; it was to correct them and direct them again in his steps. Look at what God said to Abraham after he had his son Ishmael with Hagar:

"God also said to Abraham, 'As for Sarai your wife, you are no longer to call her Sarai; her name will be Sarah. I will bless her and will surely give you a son by her. I will bless her so that she will be the mother of nations; kings of peoples will come from her.'

"Abraham fell facedown; he laughed and said to himself, 'Will a son be born to a man a hundred years old? Will Sarah bear a child at the age of ninety?' And Abraham said to God, 'If only Ishmael might live under your blessing!'

"Then God said, 'Yes, but your wife Sarah will bear you a son, and you will call him Isaac. I will establish my covenant with him as an everlasting covenant for his descendants after him. And as for Ishmael, I have heard you: I will surely bless him; I will make him fruitful and will greatly increase his numbers. He will be the father of twelve rulers, and I will make him into a great nation. But my covenant I will establish with Isaac, whom Sarah will bear to you by this time next year.' When he had finished speaking with Abraham, God went up from him" (Gen. 17:15–22).

God reminded Abraham of his plan. Things had not changed in God's mind, in spite of the lack of faith and missteps of Abraham and Sarah. The incident with Hagar would not be the only mistake Abraham and Sarah would make. But God was patient and faithful to fulfill what he promised to them. What happens through the course of twenty-five years between the moment God first tells Abraham what he will do and the time of its fulfillment is the strengthening of Abraham's faith. I've called this a journey from fear to faith because the road to a strong faith and trust in God isn't an overnight thing. Some of God's most ardent followers in the Bible struggled to believe at times. Fear and doubt plagued the best of them. Moral failures overshadowed them. But the universal reason each of them was successful in being used by God for his purposes was that none of them gave up on God. They continued to stay faithful to him, even when they didn't fully understand what he was doing. They allowed his correction in their lives when they missed the mark. And they were convinced that he wouldn't give up on them, because he is a God of grace.

At the fulfillment of God's promise to Abraham that he would be the father of the great nation of Israel, Abraham's faith was strong and unwavering. Rather than his faith weakening in the midst of his mistakes and the delay of the promise, Abraham allowed his faith to grow stronger until he was fully convinced that, in spite of the impossibility, he and Sarah would indeed be parents. Look what Romans says about Abraham's faith at the end of his journey:

"Against all hope, Abraham in hope believed and so became the father of many nations, just as it had been said to him, 'So shall your offspring be.' Without weakening in his faith, he faced the fact that his body was as good as dead—since he was about a hundred years old—and that Sarah's womb was also dead. Yet he did not waver through unbelief regarding the promise of God, but was strengthened in his faith and gave glory to God, being fully persuaded that God had power to do what he had promised" (Rom. 4:18–22).

Remember what grace is? It is the power of God at work in us to accomplish what we couldn't do without it. The grace of God strengthened

Abraham's faith. God's strength is made perfect or complete in our weakness. And Abraham, after twenty-five years of waiting, was fully persuaded that God's power would accomplish what had been promised.

One of my favorite Bible passages regarding this idea of grace is found in Psalm 37:

"If the LORD delights in a man's way, he makes his steps firm; though he stumble, he will not fall, for the LORD upholds him with his hand" (Ps. 37:23–24).

When I read these verses, I imagine a proud parent watching her one-year-old beginning to walk. Walking is a required task for that little one to learn that he will need throughout his life. But it is not something that anyone gets right the first time. Or the second time, for that matter. When that child takes a step and stumbles, does the parent get upset? Does she blame or punish the child for stumbling? Of course not! It is understood by the parent that this is a process that will take some time. And it is in the trial and error that the child will learn and grow in his ability to walk. When the child stumbles, the parent grabs the child by the hands and helps him get steady again so he can continue trying to walk.

I believe that is the picture the Lord is giving us in Psalm 37 regarding our journey of faith. We're not going to get it right all the time, especially not right away. When we stumble, God is not going to blame or punish us, because he knows we are trying to do what we're supposed to. When God knows that, he takes delight in us, just like a proud parent takes delight in her child's efforts to walk. When we do stumble or take a misstep, God grabs our hand and helps us get steady on our spiritual feet again. He makes our steps firm. God's intent is to not let us utterly fall. He is passionate about our success, just like any good parent who passionately wants her children to succeed in life. You matter so much to God, and your life is so significant to him. You are his child.

Free to Risk

It is impossible to explore the matter of faith and trust in God without addressing the topic of risk. Faith requires that we believe without seeing, that we act in accordance to faith without being certain of results.

That, my friend, is risky! People who accomplish great things have a certain tolerance for risk. First and foremost, they recognize that the reward of accomplishment far exceeds the cost of risk. They also know that failure is not the end of the matter. As we just discussed, grace removes the fear of failure. It allows risk taking, because with grace, there are second chances.

Now this isn't some crazy, foolhardy risk taking that is for one's own thrill-seeking or glory. This is the risk that comes along with stepping out in faith in an area we've never tried before. And this stepping out has been prompted by an invitation from the Lord, similar to what happened to Peter when Jesus asked him to step out of the boat during the storm and walk to him on the water. That would have been foolhardy had Jesus not asked Peter to do it. However, because it was at Jesus's request, it was a matter of faith, trust, and, yes, risk!

Peter could have rationalized in his mind that water-walking was OK for Jesus, because, after all, he was Jesus! He had already turned water into wine, healed blind eyes, and raised people from the dead. Walking on water would be right up his miracle alley! But for Peter, it was a different story. There were perilous waves all around that no seasoned fisherman would dare to take on under normal circumstances. If Jesus didn't supernaturally help Peter, drowning would have been an imminent possibility. And there was the matter of Peter's reputation with the rest of the disciples if this didn't work. If he was wrong about this, he'd probably never live it down!

Peter could hear them now: *Way to go, Peter! What in the world made you think you could walk on water? You're not Jesus, you know! For cryin' out loud, you just about got yourself killed. Do you see any of us trying something that crazy?* But the reality is, because of faith, Peter did something none of the other disciples would ever do. He walked on water. And as long as he kept his eyes on Jesus, Peter could do the impossible. It was only when Peter let fear and doubt back in that he began to sink. Yet, once again, God revealed his amazing grace in Peter's moment of fear and failure. As he sank and cried out in fear, Jesus grabbed him by the hand and lifted him up. Sound familiar?

"[T]hough he stumbles, he will not fall, for the Lord upholds him with his hand" (Ps. 37:24b).

That lesson would help Peter grow in his faith and to be one of the pillars of the Christian church. His life would be an example throughout history of a man who was radically transformed by the love and grace of Christ. Thousands would be saved by his preaching, supernatural healing would flow from him to set people free, and countless lives would be encouraged through his powerful New Testament teachings. All because he was willing to risk and follow hard after Christ, whether he did things right all the time or not. That can be you, my friend. Grace has got you covered.

I love this quote by Theodore Roosevelt:

It is not the critic who counts; not the man who points out how the strong man stumbles, or where the doer of deeds could have done them better. The credit belongs to the man who is actually in the arena, whose face is marred by dust and sweat and blood; who strives valiantly; who errs, who comes short again and again, because there is no effort without error and shortcoming; but who does actually strive to do the deeds; who knows great enthusiasms, the great devotions; who spends himself in a worthy cause; who at the best knows in the end the triumph of high achievement, and who at the worst, if he fails, at least fails while daring greatly, so that his place shall never be with those cold and timid souls who neither know victory nor defeat.

5

NOBODY'S PERFECT!

Many years ago, I read a book called *Tired of Trying to Measure Up* by Jeff VanVonderen. It struck a very personal chord with me. I grew up struggling to believe I could ever be good enough at whatever I did. It didn't matter if it was academics, athletics, or pleasing my parents. I lived under a constant fear of criticism and, as a result, developed a perfectionistic mentality that followed me into adulthood.

When most people hear that someone is a perfectionist, they tend to assume that the person just has very high standards and performs tasks exceptionally well. If that were the case, then certainly perfectionism would be a good thing. After all, why would having high standards be a problem? When was the last time a friend with a medical concern asked you if you knew of any mediocre doctors he or she could go to? The problem isn't that perfectionists have high standards; it's that they have *unrealistic* standards. The bar is set too high.

For most perfectionists, good is never good enough. *Very* good is never good enough, especially if someone else can do it better. They have a knack for disqualifying even the very best of their efforts. For example, if a perfectionist gets a B-plus for a class grade, he will say to himself, "I should have gotten an A. If only I had just worked a little harder."

However, if the same individual got an A, he might think, "I didn't really work hard enough to get an A," or "The class was an easy one. Lots of people got As," and discredit his accomplishment.

The Fear of Failure

Some personality types display a tendency toward a different type of perfectionism. They have an internal drive to be the best at whatever they do. However, they are driven by a competitive nature, not insecurity. For them, the motivation is the thrill of achievement and accomplishment. Rather than feeling like they never measure up, these folks believe that they can do whatever they put their minds to. They are confident and often excel at the things they do.

The perfectionism I'm talking about is when striving to do well is driven by fear—the fear of failure, the fear of not measuring up, the fear of being rejected by others if one's performance isn't good enough. It is rooted in insecurity, not confidence. It's a terrible weight to live with. Every accomplishment comes with a high price tag. Sadly, the reward from accomplishment feels small, because it is often perceived by the perfectionist as undeserved.

David Seamonds, in his book *Healing for Damaged Emotions*, describes this experience in terms of a person climbing a ladder, and just when he thinks he's reached the top rung, there is always one more rung. A person who struggles with these beliefs is set up for constant failure. When standards are unrealistic, failure is inevitable, which causes the perfectionist to feel he is in a state of perpetual failure. Many perfectionists will then give up trying and let things in their lives fall apart. Or they don't bother trying anything new, eliminating the possibility of more failure. Because of these tendencies, some are labeled lazy or apathetic—the opposite of what they really are.

The Constant Voice of Criticism

One client who I worked with who battled perfectionism described her life as one giant stressor. Growing up, she had been criticized and held to an unrealistic standard by a perfectionistic and demanding parent, which laid the foundation for a life of insecurity and unrelenting feelings of never being good enough. As a child, she came to believe that she had to be whatever others wanted her to be. Her opinion didn't matter. These beliefs carried over into her adulthood.

Every day she heard voices in her head telling her what she was doing wrong. No area of her life was exempt from the critical voices. Her work life was bombarded with messages like, "You're not doing enough. You should be working harder. You're not going to succeed. You need to be more motivated." As a wife, the messages were, "You're not being a devoted wife. You're not meeting your husband's needs. You're the problem in the marriage." Ironically, her husband was an alcoholic who had an affair and was virtually disconnected from both his wife and their children. In most troubled marriages, there are contributing factors from both spouses, but clearly her beliefs were significantly skewed and imbalanced. Parenting was no different, as she was plagued by thoughts like, "You're too lenient with your kids. You don't correct them properly. You're going to mess them up." She shared with me that many days all she wanted to do was stay in bed. Who wouldn't want to stay in bed if she had to face those kinds of messages every day? No wonder some perfectionists want to give up or develop significant anxiety and depression!

As I began working with her on her beliefs about herself, she started having a more balanced view of who she really was, and the transformation was amazing. She reevaluated her critical views of herself regarding parenting and started seeing all the things that she was doing right. Perfectionists often don't trust their own judgment, so it is a major milestone of healing to be able to be confident in one's own ability to evaluate and decide what is right.

She also prioritized what was most important to her in being a successful parent and realized she was actually a pretty good mom! She loved her kids and did all she could to help them know they were loved, safe, and secure. She readily admitted there were areas she could improve on, but as she was able to be fairer to herself, the stress of parenting lifted significantly. As a result, she began enjoying her kids more—or perhaps more accurately, she enjoyed her mom role more, because it no longer carried such a heavy sense of failure. Being a mom brought the joy that God intended it to bring.

The Need to Control

Another symptom I see in perfectionistic clients is excessive attempts to control everything and everyone. As all of us know, there are too many things in our lives that are really out of our control, so the attempt to micromanage people, circumstances, and events to always try to appear in the best light possible is a waste of time and energy. It is a losing battle. One of the biggest areas of control for perfectionists is in the area of image control.

Whether it is image control of themselves, their spouse, or their kids, how everyone "appears" to outsiders is critical. Kids have to be on their best behavior at all times in public. The spouse needs to display a certain image, whatever the perfectionist deems important. Usually there are lots of family secrets that no one is allowed to tell. No one can really know what's "wrong" in the family. Each family member feels the pressure to give the impression that everything is good in their lives. But ultimately the hypocrisy and secret keeping takes its toll as serious problems are never really resolved. Eventually, things begin to break down and the dysfunction shows up in public ways as problems at work, school, health, and so on.

I live in the Minneapolis area, and in 2007, one of our major bridges, the I-35W, collapsed during rush hour, causing cars to fall into the Mississippi River and trapping many passengers inside their vehicles. All told, thirteen people died and 145 were injured. It was considered one of the worst bridge disasters in US history. After a yearlong investigation, it was discovered that there was a design flaw in the metal plates that connect the steel beams together on the bridge. Something foundational to the structure of the bridge was faulty. The bridge was able to function for a number of years, but after a while, the constant stress of thousands, if not millions, of cars driving over it eventually revealed the structure deficit, and the bridge collapsed. The bridge looked good but had a serious problem with its structure that, given enough time, would cause its eventual destruction. So it is with families that have problems within their structures. They may look good on the outside for a while, weathering the stresses of day-to-day life, but eventually, the stresses will be too much and will reveal the problems that exist. They won't stay hidden forever. Control and hiding things will only work so long.

Pleasing and Appeasing

Another trait I'd like to address is that of people-pleasing. Perfectionists may develop the tendency to be chameleons—changing who they are to be more pleasing to others. It is another attempt to be "good enough." Oftentimes people who have this tendency describe the experience as losing who they really are. They battle a deep fear of rejection, which fuels the people-pleasing. Eventually, they start to feel anger and resentment because of the lack of any true reward for all their efforts to please others.

Excessive Analysis

What are they thinking about me? Did I say/do the wrong thing? Did I look/sound stupid in that exchange with so-and-so?

Ever have these kinds of conversations with yourself? I have. Many times. And the conversations didn't end well. They ended with me imagining the worst possible outcome. As a former (or mostly recovered) perfectionist, the need to evaluate my effect on other people was huge. Because I was constantly striving for approval so I could feel OK about myself, I invariably felt I had to analyze almost everything I did to decide if I did "it" well enough, whatever "it" was. As someone with a calling that includes public teaching and speaking, that kind of personal scrutiny was torturous. I was certainly my own worst critic. I have many memories of having a panic attack before a speaking engagement, wondering if I had prepared well enough or if the talk would be interesting and effective. Then I would have a panic attack after the talk! I would break down in tears, imagining how badly I *might* have messed up. My husband would look at me like I was crazy. I would get wonderful responses from people, but in spite of them, I would analyze myself into a panic-stricken funk.

Insecurity doesn't make you very objective. And in reality, it didn't matter if month after month, year after year, people would tell me how much they loved and appreciated my teaching and speaking. It was like the positive affirmations were going into a cavernous black hole, because at the core of perfectionism is a deeply entrenched belief that "I'm never good enough." Every compliment, every positive affirmation slams into the brick wall of disbelief. In the end, I had to deal with the false belief. I had to choose to get rid of it and allow myself to believe the truth. I'll address this more in chapter 8, where I talk about getting rid of stinkin' thinkin'. The wonderful, healing thing about believing the truth that you are OK and good enough just as you are is that no one can convince you that you aren't! Compliments and criticisms no longer define you. Of course that understanding doesn't mean we can't grow, improve, and change in some areas. It just means we believe God's truth that we are wonderfully made and don't have to live by unrealistic expectations.

One of the great joys I experience in helping people overcome perfectionism is seeing them become comfortable in their own skin. I see their true personalities come out. They laugh more. They look more peaceful. And their God-given creativity begins to flourish. I will often hear them tell me that people close to them tell them that how glad they are to see the "real" person emerge.

Roots of Perfectionism

How does perfectionism develop? It can develop from growing up in a home where affirmations are rare and the child is criticized frequently.

Perfectionistic parents produce perfectionistic children. Unhealthy standards and unrealistic expectations can be passed down from one generation to another. Often this fear is developed when punishment for mistakes is too harsh. The child learns that mistakes and failures are not tolerated. Therefore, only perfect behavior or performance is acceptable. A natural result is insecurity and a fear of failure. They will begin to expect punishment or rejection for failure. The internal pressure to meet others' expectations all the time becomes an emotional and psychological slave driver.

Criticism from other significant people like teachers or coaches can also fuel perfectionistic tendencies. Perhaps a teacher criticized you for being a poor speller, and now as an adult you hate to do any kind of writing for fear of looking stupid. Or maybe a coach humiliated you for a silly mistake, and as a result, the thought of athletic competition puts knots in your stomach. Fear does some crazy things to us. Criticism, humiliation, and shame for failures can sometimes take the most capable people and render them powerless.

Performance Anxiety vs. Perfectionism

In life, we all feel some performance anxiety from time to time. Who doesn't get a little nervous right before a big exam or an important sporting event? Or how about having a few jitters before a job interview? In fact, some research shows that a little anxiety, with its release of adrenaline, can actually help us perform better. (Note: I said *a little*!) But for perfectionists, fear and insecurity rears their ugly heads with each new task. The anxiety actually has the opposite effect and causes the person to underperform, thereby creating a self-fulfilling prophecy of "I'm not good enough." Anxiety is always high, and adrenaline and stress hormones are being released in regularly high quantities, creating long-term stress response in the mind and body, which in turn can create stress-related illnesses in the body.

God does not want us to live under the constant pressure of unrealistically high expectations of ourselves. God knows we are imperfect. None of us can do everything perfectly. It's just not possible.

If you struggle with perfectionism, begin to identify where you may be expecting more from yourself than is fair. Do you expect more from yourself than you would other people? Do you constantly worry about what other people think about you? Are you constantly trying to do image control? Do you obsess about how you or your family appears to others? Let it go. God wants you to be yourself. No one's standard for your life matters but God's. He made you a masterpiece. He made you with special gifts and abilities, but you can't be everything, know everything, and do everything. Do an honest inventory of all that you do well. What are your strengths? Focus on them, value them. Extend yourself the same grace God extends to you. You don't have to be perfect.

6

BECOMING CONFIDENT IN WHO YOU ARE

"No one can make you feel inferior without your
consent."

—ELEANOR ROOSEVELT

There's a term in psychology that has gotten a bad rap in some Christian
circles. It's the term "self-esteem." In general, those who have had an issue
with it felt it showed a focus on "self" instead of God.

I would like to take a look at the idea of self-esteem from a different
angle. Esteem is how something is regarded in terms of its value or worth.
We give or judge the value of things all the time. There is nothing unchristian about that. It's a normal thing to do. At its basic root, self-esteem is
the value or worth a person places on him or herself. The fact is, every
person establishes some estimation of his personal worth, and by personal
worth, I mean worth as a human being. The standards of measurement we
use are often determined by the culture's estimation of talents, abilities,
influence, and adequacy. We all place value on these in varying degrees
and use the scale that we establish in our minds as a means of evaluating

ourselves and others. Of course there are subcultures within the broader culture that play into what we value. For example, specific families establish their own value systems within their culture. If a family has a lot of naturally athletic members, being good at sports may have a higher value than, say, artistic ability. Academic achievement may be a priority in other families. The schools people attend may shape and mold certain values. Religious affiliations also influence a person's value system. So the value systems and standards a person is exposed to over the course of his life will determine what type of value he places on himself.

There are so many possible standards for worth coming from the cultural influences around us that it can be incredibly difficult to accurately assess one's own personal worth. Let's say you were born into a family where both parents were accomplished athletes, but you don't have an athletic bone in your body. How do you establish your own sense of value and worth? If you're lucky, you will have lived in an environment where many different types of abilities were recognized and valued.

But for many people, broad acceptance of varying abilities isn't part of their experience, and as a result, they live under a constant cloud of self-doubt and insecurity. Sadly, I've seen incredibly talented, gifted women who feel lousy about themselves because they feel they aren't thin enough. They are bombarded by the culture's value of thinness, and they place all their emphasis on that one value to the exclusion of myriad other abilities that are infinitely more important. People live under an intense weight of dissatisfaction about who they are. So how do we establish a value system that recognizes the true worth of a human being?

As Christians, we believe God created humankind and that he has established our worth. Our estimation of our own worth should come from what he values. So if we are to have a healthy, balanced self-esteem, we need to see ourselves as God sees us and establish our value system based on the truth found in God's word. There are several traps people can fall into in regard to accurately estimating their personal worth. The first is the comparison trap.

The Comparison Trap

Although Christians acknowledge that they are made by God, they often have very low estimations of their own worth. They compare themselves to others who they feel are more talented and dismiss or devalue what they have to offer.

I think Satan has used comparison and the resulting insecurity as a huge weapon against God's people, particularly women. Women are masters at comparing themselves to other women. It can be a relentless obsession, and the by-product is perpetual insecurity. Men certainly aren't immune to this, but it would seem it is an especially destructive tendency in women. Eating disorders, self-injury, jealousy, anxiety, and depression are just a few of the symptoms of low self-esteem that can develop from perceived inadequacies that come from constant comparison.

If we compare ourselves to other people, we are using the wrong standard. No two human beings are completely alike. The human race consists of an infinite number of combinations of personality traits, abilities, and life experiences that make each of us uniquely who we are. To compare oneself with anyone else, even to someone with similar traits, would be like comparing apples to oranges. So much potential is wasted in very capable people because of their deep sense of inadequacy.

Bill Hybels, senior pastor of Willow Creek Church in Chicago, gives an interesting illustration in his book *Descending into Greatness* of how chickens establish what's called the "pecking order":

Take ten chickens. Any ten. Put them in a pen together, and spread a little chicken feed. In short order, you will witness an amazing phenomenon. In a matter of minutes, the chickens, previously strangers, will form a hierarchy based on dominance; or, in every-day language, they will establish a Pecking Order. Instinctively, they will determine, through a series of skirmishes, who the Number One Chicken will be, then the Number Two; the Number Three; all the way down to the unlucky Number Ten Chicken. Much is at stake in this dance of domination. Chicken Number One pecks at and intimidates Chicken Number Two, without experiencing any kind of retribution from Chicken Number Two. Chicken Number Two will take it from Chicken Number One but will turn around and peck away at Chicken Number Three, who will, in turn, take out its frustration on Chicken Number Four. The Pecking Order continues all the way down to Chicken Number Ten, who needless to say, has a pretty miserable life: pecked, but no one to peck.[1]

I think all of us to some degree create pecking orders in our minds in relation to how we see people. We may have different ranking systems, but consciously or subconsciously, we decide who is the most powerful, influential, successful, knowledgeable, and so forth. Next we decide where we fall in the ranks. How do we measure up? At our jobs, Chicken Number One may be our boss, or perhaps one of our coworkers who is the favorite of the boss. At church, the top chickens may be those who hold certain titles or ministry positions. Sadly, we may look at others with less prestigious roles and designate them "Chicken Number Ten." Think about the crazy evaluations that go on at high school reunions: Who's going bald or has the most gray hair? Who gained the most weight? Who has the best job and makes the most money? We may get nervous thinking about meeting our old high school flame, wondering how we compare to the person he married.

Oftentimes, when we establish who the most important people in the pecking order are, we begin to feel intimidated by them if we are not at their level. One definition of intimidation is "to make one timid or fearful." Has anyone ever made you feel timid? Uncomfortable because of the esteem you held for them?

I have been intimidated by people many times. It was always people I respected; I worried that I would somehow look or act stupid when I was around them. I was afraid they would reject me or disrespect me because I wasn't up to a certain standard in their eyes. I would literally become timid in their presence, sometimes hardly able to put a sentence together! Ironically, most of them were very nice people who would never have wanted me to feel that way around them. Nor did they do anything to me to make me feel that way. I had just evaluated them at such a higher level than myself and, as a result, made myself feel inferior. Comparison does some ugly things. It is OK to respect and regard people highly, but not to the extent that it makes us feel insecure about who we are.

There will always be someone who is better than you at some skills, perhaps smarter or more educated. But no one on earth can possess the special combination of attributes that you have. No one. And this world will be denied something very important that you alone can offer it. As Marilyn Monroe once said, "Wanting to be someone else is a waste of the person you are."

The "I'm a Nothing" Trap

Unfortunately, there has been a subtle twist on the theology of our sinful condition that can also fuel our sense of inadequacy or worthlessness. It is the thought that we are nothing without Christ. Examine the teaching of Christ that says we can *do* nothing without him: "I am the vine; you are the branches. If a man remains in me and I in him, he will bear much fruit; apart from me you can do nothing" (John 15:5).

We have taken this and twisted it to say we *are* nothing. There is a very familiar worship chorus that says, "I am nothing without you." God didn't create any of us as "nothings." In fact, the Bible says we are all created in God's image, with intellect, reason, creativity, emotion, and spiritual gifts. James teaches that we should not use our mouths to curse men, because they have been made in God's likeness (James 3:9–10).

Our God-given traits can be tainted by sin, but they are not worthless traits. They are traits that will be redeemed by Christ to bring out their intended value. Can you imagine going to a baby dedication at church and hearing the pastor say, "This baby only has value in Christ; it is nothing without Christ"? I realize that sounds absurd, but in reality, it's a belief many Christians embrace. It may sound like humility, but it is in fact insecurity shrouded in a spiritual veneer. True humility is having an accurate estimation of oneself that is determined by God and his word. The Bible says that while we were still sinners, Christ died for us *because* we have value to him (Rom. 5:8). Christ didn't die for a bunch of nothings. David describes the remarkable status and value God has placed on mankind in Psalm 8:

"When I consider your heavens, the work of your fingers, the moon and the stars, which you have set in place, what is man that you are mindful of him, the son of man that you care for him? You made him a little lower than the heavenly beings and crowned him with glory and honor" (Ps. 8:3–5).

When I read David's words, I can almost picture him sitting and imagining the splendor of the universe, a beautiful radiant moon and a vast expanse of sky flooded with millions of stars. As he tries to comprehend the magnificence of what he has seen so many nights, he wonders how man can compare to the greatness of the heavenly universe. Yet he comes to this God-revealed conclusion: Man has been given a glory that exceeds the stars in the universe. David asks, "What is man, that you are mindful of him and care about him?" It blows his mind that God would esteem man to the extent of classifying him as only a little lower than all the heavenly beings. David recognizes that God has placed a special glory and honor on man.

Several years ago, I heard Dr. Mark Rutland, former president of both Oral Roberts University and Southeastern University in Florida, speak at a Christian conference. He told a story of how he had experienced excruciating foot pain one time just prior to preaching at a church that had invited him to speak. He had been lying on a pew alone, well before the service was to start, agonizing not only about the pain, but also about how he was going to "hobble" up to the podium to speak on divine healing!

Very shortly after, a young man named Jimmy came running into the sanctuary with his ten-gallon cowboy hat, cowboy boots, and guns blazing, shouting, "Bang, bang! Bang, bang!"

Jimmy was not an exuberant five-year-old playing Wild West. Jimmy was a young man with Down syndrome. Dr. Rutland was not exactly thrilled at the interruption during this rather inopportune moment. Jimmy went to see what the matter was with "Brother Mark"—or "Bwudda Mawk," as Jimmy called him. When Dr. Rutland explained his painful foot problem, Jimmy very compassionately prayed a simple prayer: "Dear Jesus, please heal Bwudda Mawk's foot."

Immediately, Dr. Rutland's foot was healed. There are several things I've always loved about this story, but one sticks out to me in this moment. God's glory and honor rest on the Jimmys of the world. Jesus loves them and gave his life for them because they are valuable. And he can use their lives to do miraculous things. I have no doubt that Jimmy has touched many people's lives.

I read this sobering statistic regarding Down syndrome–related abortions. In the United States, a number of studies have estimated that the abortion rate of babies with Down syndrome ranges from 87 percent to 98 percent, depending on the study. Abortion rates in Europe following a prenatal diagnosis of Down syndrome were between 91 percent and 93 percent, according to a 2002 literature review. As I read this, I wondered, what if Jimmy hadn't been born? God sees value in every human being, regardless of gender, ethnicity, physical or mental limitations, or age. Each life bears the glory of God. And God can use any life that is surrendered to him.

Have you battled the feeling that you're a nothing or that God can't use you? It's not true. *You* bear God's glory. You have been made in his image and he not only *can* use your life, he *wants* to use it. Stop believing the lie and let God use your life!

God's Objective Evaluation

When God shows us who and what we really are to him, we know what is of value in our lives and what isn't. We are able to recognize our gifts, strengths, and God-given abilities. We know, just as David wrote in Psalm 139:14, that we are fearfully and wonderfully made, and for that reason, we can praise God, our creator. At the same time, God can show us how ugly our sin and selfishness are, and we can recognize their lack of value and, as a result, choose to repent and change.

John Ortberg, in his book *The Me I Want to Be: Becoming God's Best Version of You*, writes, "Low self-esteem causes me to believe that I have so little worth that my response does not matter. With repentance, however, I understand that being worth so much to God is why my response is so important."

The only worthless thing about you is your sin and selfishness. Everything else about you is worth the sacrifice of the perfect life of the son of God. Your life was redeemed at an incredibly high price. It doesn't make sense that God would pay a high price for something of little value.

Having a balanced view of ourselves also means we can accept the fact that we have weaknesses and vulnerabilities. Those are not necessarily sins, just the normal imperfections of humanity. They are the traits that God's grace makes up for. Christ's strength is made perfect in our weakness.

The "Someone Else Can Do It Better" Trap

Have you ever had someone in your life who brought out the best in you? Perhaps it was a coach, teacher, parent, or pastor. That person could see potential in you that you couldn't see and seemed to know just how to help you believe in yourself.

I had just such an experience with my high school tennis coach. I was a varsity tennis player, and during one singles match, I was down two games to nine. We were playing ten-game sets, so all my opponent had to do was win one more game to beat me. The odds were clearly stacked against me. My confidence was gone, and I was expecting a crushing defeat. My coach, whom I had a great deal of respect for, walked by my court and asked me what the score was. I told her the score, and I will never forget her next question. She said, "Why is she beating you? You're better than her." It was like a switch flipped in me in that moment. My coach saw in me what I couldn't see, but more importantly, she helped me believe in myself. I proceeded to win the next nine games and beat my opponent 11–9.

You have a God who knows all of your abilities and potential, and he believes in you. But no matter what God believes about you, it won't make any difference if you don't believe in yourself. God will even ask you to do things you don't believe you can do so that you can discover your potential. He wouldn't ask you if you couldn't. God really wants you to believe in yourself. The problem is, we don't always respect his opinion like we ought to. Instead, we argue with him and make excuses as to why we can't.

Moses tried that once with God, the arguing and excuse-making bit. God shows up in a burning bush and asks Moses to lead his people out of Egypt. God was going to do supernatural things through Moses to establish his leadership. Moses had the goods, and God knew it. The problem was, Moses looked at what he believed was a great weakness, his speech impediment, and concluded that he couldn't do the job. He thought someone else would be more qualified. So Moses argued with God, and God got mad. On some level, it was insulting to God for Moses to tell him that he wasn't qualified to do something God clearly felt he could do. Perfect speech wasn't a prerequisite for being a great leader. God created Moses.

And God reminded Moses that he made his mouth—and everything else about him, for that matter! If anyone would know what Moses had the ability to do, it was the one who made him. God had Aaron speak for Moses, and Moses led millions of people successfully.

God Wants You to Believe in Yourself

God wants you to believe in yourself and your abilities. To deny their existence is to deny God and his handiwork. When you believe in who God made you to be, you fulfill your purpose, and joy is the result. God is pleased with us when we are free to be the people he created us to be. We are his workmanship, and he takes pride in what he makes.

In the early years of my Christian walk, I felt God calling me to teach Bible studies. It started with children and eventually included adults. With the children, I felt comfortable and discovered I really enjoyed watching their faces light up as they gained some new understanding. Adults, on the other hand, totally freaked me out. Thoughts raced through my mind: *What if I say something stupid? What if I'm boring? What if I didn't hear from God? Will they notice how nervous I am?* I would lie awake for hours the night before a speaking engagement. I would compare myself to other speakers who I thought were more gifted than I was. In spite of my fear, I knew God had called me to teach and speak. It was confirmed over and over as people would tell me how my teaching had impacted them. More than anything, I wanted to obey the Lord, but I was pretty convinced that obeying him was going to cause me to die young of a stress-related illness!

At some point, I knew that wasn't how God wanted me to feel as I used my gifts to fulfill his purposes for my life. I had many heart-to-heart talks with the Lord. The Lord told me essentially the same thing he told Peter in regard to walking on water: "You've got to take your eyes off of the natural circumstances (your abilities, people's responses, being the center of attention), and look at me. Know you are doing this for me, and I will take care of the results. If I anoint you, it doesn't matter what your abilities are or are not. You don't have to be like anyone else who speaks and teaches." As I let those words of truth penetrate my heart, I began speaking and teaching with greater confidence and peace. I let go of worrying about what others were going to think of me, and instead I focused on what God thought of me. If he was pleased with my obedience, that was all that mattered. I began feeling joy in using my gifts instead of fear. I realized the more I trusted God and let him work through me, the more my speaking impacted others.

Perhaps you feel God has been calling you to do something that seems scary to you: working with children, reaching out to mend a broken relationship, sharing your faith, starting a new ministry, or writing a book. You haven't done it yet because you've been too afraid. You've been questioning your abilities. Or perhaps you're waiting for God to show up in a burning bush to remove all of your doubt and uncertainty (remember how well the bush worked for Moses!).

The truth is, God has gifted you and believes in you. Respect God's opinion of you. Let it build your confidence. You may recognize weaknesses in yourself like Moses did, but that only means you have to keep your eyes on God. You will need to depend on him. Lean on him.

I was recently reading the book *Prophet* by R. J. Larson. It's a fantasy novel about a young seventeen-year-old girl named Ela who has been called by her creator, the Infinite, to be his prophet. Her young, innocent-hearted sister, Tzana, is used by the Infinite to help reveal the "gift" of her new calling. Tzana is very excited about what is happening to her sister until she sees the fear on her sister's face.

She says to Ela, "I thought this would make you happy. It's a gift from the Infinite."

Ela, filled with insecurity, responds a lot like Moses did:

"Infinite," Ela babbled into her cupped hands, "here I am—and I don't know why! Who has ever heard of a girl becoming a prophet? I'm clumsy and insignificant. No one will listen to me. And I dropped like a stone when You shared a vision with me. I'm not going to be of any use to You at all!"

"You will. If you accept."

She drank in the words and sat up, thinking hard. She had two choices. Live to be old, silver-haired, and full of dry regrets, or accept this 'gift' with all its uncertainties. Listening to the Infinite.[2]

Accept God's gifts. Listen to the Infinite.

Waiting on God or Procrastination?

In his book *Seizing Your Divine Moment*, Erwin McManus writes:

Don't wait to begin using your spiritual gifts until you understand all the details about how they will be expressed in your life. Don't look for God to fill in all the blanks. Don't wait for Him to remove all the uncertainty. Realize He may actually increase the uncertainty and leverage all the odds against you, just so you will know in the end that it wasn't your gifts but His power through your gifts that fulfilled His purpose in your life.[3]

Sometimes waiting on God is really just procrastination due to fear. You can wait forever until everything feels "safe" or until you feel completely confident. However, you will lose opportunity after opportunity to do something in this life that makes a difference for eternity. God has designed you for a wonderful purpose. There will always be struggles and obstacles, successes and failures. But in the end, a life fully surrendered to the purposes of God will accomplish much.

High in the King's Estimate

A poor but devout Frenchman came to his spiritual advisor and said with a sorrowing heart: "I profess faith in God, but at times, against my will, I'm overwhelmed with doubts as I try to live a Christian life in this world. Surely, God must be displeased with me as I struggle to overcome them."

The clergyman answered with much kindness, "The King of France has two castles in different areas and sends a commander to each of them. The castle of Mantleberry stands in a place remote from danger, far inland; but the castle of La Rochelle is on the coast, where it is liable to continued sieges. Now which of the two commanders, do you think, stands highest in the estimate of the King—the commander of La Rochelle, or he of Mantleberry?"

"Doubtless," said the poor man, "the King values him the most who has the hardest task, and braves the greatest dangers."

"You are right," replied his advisor, "And now apply this matter to your case and mine."[4]

7

FROM CHICKEN TO HERO

As a kid, I was always a bit shy and self-conscious. I hated being the center of attention. Whether it was sharing in front of the class at school or participating in band concerts and sporting events, I dreaded the thought of being watched. I was afraid of doing or saying something stupid. I would get embarrassed easily, and as you might imagine, junior high provided plenty of opportunities for public humiliation at the hands of insensitive classmates. On the self-confidence meter, I was somewhere around a negative two.

Throughout the years I haven't exactly been a daredevil either. While many kids look forward to spending summer days at amusement parks, waiting in line with great anticipation of riding the "Flight of Fear" roller coaster, I would stand in line, palms sweating, stomach in knots, ready to pass out at the thought of what the next few minutes would hold on the steel monster. Rather than screaming as I rode, I would hold my breath until I couldn't hold it in anymore and then whimper faintly. When we were done, everyone else would be chattering excitedly about how great the ride was, but all I could do was stare blankly at the others and try to keep from throwing up on their shoes. I was the chicken of the group, and I knew it.

I Wanna Be a Hero

Of course, I always wanted to be brave. I would often imagine myself as one of the brave heroes in the movies who fought powerful villains and saved everyone, or the underdog who overcame great adversity to become a champion. I didn't play with dolls much, but when I did, my Barbie was always a gold medalist in the Olympics. I would put a one-piece swimsuit on her and pretend she was a world-class gymnast or high-dive champion. My friends and I would spend hours running makeshift obstacle courses, pretending we were track stars. I believe all of us have a desire deep down to be a hero.

The Bible is full of heroes. Not the type with capes and masks or the type that gets gold medals, just ordinary folks who courageously lived life in the face of tremendous difficulties. There is a whole chapter in the book of Hebrews dedicated to some of these incredibly brave men and women.

All of them stood up for what was right, regardless of the consequences—consequences that included being stoned, killed by a sword, or eaten by lions. Some were tortured. All of them were courageous, regardless of the cost. The one universal trait that they all possessed besides courage was strong faith. A faith that was worth living and dying for. And the source of their faith was a God who loved them and gave them a hope for something vastly better beyond the horrible circumstances they faced.

As you might guess, given my chicken mentality, I can't imagine what it would be like to face possible torture and death for taking a stand for what is right. That kind of bravery blows my mind. Hero status has always felt far beyond my reach.

Then one day I discovered someone in the Bible who reminded me a lot of myself. His name was Gideon. I say this with no disrespect, but he was a bit of a chicken, too. However, he was also a hero of faith. Could that be possible? Yep. You can find his name in the Faith Hero Hall of

Fame in Hebrews 11. So how exactly does a person go from chicken to a hero of faith?

From Chicken to Hero

God's people, the Israelites, were in a sorry state. They were under constant oppression from their enemies the Midianites, who had plundered everything of value from them, including weapons for fighting. Everyone was discouraged, including Gideon, who believed God had abandoned Israel completely. So Gideon hid out in a winepress, threshing wheat there in hopes the Midianites wouldn't find him and take the wheat. God sent an angel to talk with Gideon:

> The angel of the LORD came and sat down under the oak in Ophrah that belonged to Joash the Abiezrite, where his son Gideon was threshing wheat in a winepress to keep it from the Midianites. When the angel of the LORD appeared to Gideon, he said, "The LORD is with you, mighty warrior."

> "But sir," Gideon replied, "if the LORD is with us, why has all this happened to us? Where are all his wonders that our fathers told us about when they said, 'Did not the LORD bring us up out of Egypt?' But now the LORD has abandoned us and put us into the hand of Midian." (Judg. 6:11–13)

Gideon did not sound very "hero-like." In fact, he sounded pretty powerless and defeated. He felt abandoned by God, and his faith was pretty much in the tank.

God decided it was time for action and gave Gideon a message through the angel: "Excuse me, O Discouraged One. Time to suck it up, and fortunately for you, I'm here to help." OK, those were my thoughts. The angel really said, "The Lord is with you, mighty warrior." I can just imagine what Gideon was thinking: *Mighty what? Uh, are you sure you have the right guy?*

Why in the world would God address Gideon that way? Because God could see what Gideon *would be* when the Lord was with him. God is Almighty (or all-mighty). It's kind of like adding infinity to any number. You get infinity. So the equation is simple:

Gideon + God = Mighty Warrior.

Have you ever thought about how God sees you when he knows he is with you? Can you imagine the possibilities for your life with God on your side? God sees great potential in us because his power is the source of our potential. God sees *what we will be* when he works through us.

You + God = Mighty Warrior.

Notice what God said next to Gideon: "The LORD turned to him and said, 'Go in the strength you have and save Israel out of Midian's hand. Am I not sending you?'

"'But Lord,' Gideon asked, 'how can I save Israel? My clan is the weakest in Manasseh, and I am the least in my family'" (Judg. 6:14–15).

Gideon's reply was not exactly oozing with faith and confidence. He was still not connecting the dots. God was telling him he had strength, God's strength, to do what he was being asked to do. But Gideon still focused only on his perceived limitations: *Don't you realize I'm a nobody, Lord, and I come from a whole family of nobodies?*

Clearly, God was not worried.

"The LORD answered, 'I will be with you, and you will strike down all the Midianites together'" (Judg. 6:16).

Now you would think that with all this powerful backing, Gideon would be a paragon of confidence. *This is a slam dunk!* Unfortunately,

Gideon was still a Nervous Nelly. God's response to Gideon was a remarkable picture of the patience of God. It is the same patience God extends toward us as we grow in our ability to believe him to work in and through us.

Gideon was still struggling to believe that God would help him defeat the Midianites, so he did the "fleece test." He set some fleece on the ground and asked God to make the fleece wet with dew and keep the ground dry to confirm his promise to Gideon. The next morning, Gideon saw that God did what he asked. Gideon, a bit more nervously, asked God to confirm it a second time, which God did. Later, God would also let Gideon know through a dream that he would give him the victory over the Midianites.

Consider the lengths God went through to convince Gideon that he was with him and Gideon would indeed be able to do the very thing he didn't think he could do. It matters greatly to God that we understand that he wants to work in and through our lives. Let me ask you a couple of questions: Has God been trying to show you that he is with you? Has he been trying to convince you that you are capable of doing _____ (you fill in the blank), but you keep arguing with him about it?

I think God created a little bit of hero in all of us that is just waiting to come out. It's time to stop believing you can't and know that if the Lord is with you, you will be able to do exactly what God is asking you to do. Change your equation from *You + 0 = You* to *You + God = Powerful You.*

Gideon would not only end up defeating the Midianites, he would do it with a small group of only three hundred men—three hundred against thousands. God intentionally stacked the odds against Gideon and his men so that they would know for certain that God himself won the victory for them. It would require them to put their faith and confidence in God alone. Look at the record of Gideon's heroics along with the other Heroes of Faith:

"And what more shall I say? I do not have time to tell about Gideon... *who through faith* conquered kingdoms, administered justice, and *gained what was promised...whose weakness was turned to strength*; and who became powerful in battle and routed foreign armies" (Heb. 11:32–34, emphasis mine).

Through faith, victories are gained and promises are obtained.

And heroes are made.

I want to tell you about one of my heroes of faith. I'll call her Betty. She was about four feet eleven and ninety-eight pounds, soaking wet. She was a quiet, hard-working mother of four who had an unshakeable faith. She was so quiet that when she spoke you had to lean down right next to her to hear her. Her husband was not a Christian and would often oppose Betty's attempts to take their children to church and invest in their spiritual growth. But Betty was determined to trust God and believe against all opposition. She was a woman of prayer and a faithful servant of the Most-High God. And God used Betty. Mightily. She persevered against years of opposition, taking her children to church, holding up godly standards in their home, and praying fervently for them. Every one of her children grew up loving Christ and serving him. Several went into vocational ministry. And eventually, after many years, her husband also committed his life to Jesus Christ. One of her daughters would become my close friend and mentor at the beginning of my Christian faith. She was not much older than me, but she had wisdom beyond her years. She would be a spiritual anchor for me during the rocky first few years of my faith. She was a product of Betty's heroic faith. Only eternity will tell how many lives were impacted for Christ through this tiny, quiet, mighty warrior.

Just recently, I read an article about another hero of faith, this time a young girl named Bethany Hamilton. Perhaps you've heard of her. Bethany began surfing at age five and was winning championships early on. She was destined to become a pro surfer. Then at age thirteen, she was attacked by a shark and lost her arm. At first, the fear of never surfing again gripped her. She had no idea what she would do without surfing. In order to fight the fear, she would get in the water and focus on catching the waves. She refused to dwell on the what-ifs. By the next year, she was competing again in national competitions and became a regular in the professional surfing circuit. She now holds a world ranking. Bethany has used her experience to be a positive role model for young girls. She also started a nonprofit organization that donates money to children who have experienced amputations. She said that one of the most beautiful things about the accident is that it has allowed her to see that she can overcome difficult things.

"I've learned life is a lot like surfing," Bethany said. "When you get caught in the impact zone, you need to get right back up, because you never know what's over the next wave...and if you have faith, anything is possible, anything at all."

Courage Isn't the Absence of Fear

Heroes come in all shapes and sizes. God may not require all of us to risk our lives standing up for what we believe or facing life-threatening dangers. Those are the hero Hall of Famers. But each of us can be everyday heroes if we are willing to recognize that by faith, we can do what we didn't think was possible. We can look fear directly in the face and overcome it with a little courage. OK, maybe a lot of courage!

I love this quote by Ambrose Redmoon: "Courage is not the absence of fear, but the judgment that something else is more important than one's fear." When I first read this quote, I began thinking about what opportunities I would miss to make a difference in this world if I continued to let fear and insecurity hold me back. You and I have the opportunity to accomplish things that have life-changing, eternal significance if we don't let fear stop us.

Charles Haddon Spurgeon was born in 1834 and became a highly influential preacher and writer of his time. He was known as the "Prince of Preachers" and, in his lifetime, preached to around ten million people. He would often preach up to ten times each week. By the time of his death in 1892, he had preached nearly thirty-six hundred sermons and published forty-nine volumes of commentaries, devotions, books on prayer, hymns, and magazines. His works are widely read and studied today. At the age of twenty-two, Spurgeon was the most popular preacher of the day, preaching to audiences numbering more than ten thousand. But along with the fame came criticism from the media that persisted throughout his life.

At the end of 1856, the year his twin sons were born, Spurgeon was preaching in the Surrey Gardens Music Hall when someone in the crowd yelled "Fire!" The crowd went into a panic and the resulting stampede left several people dead. Spurgeon was profoundly impacted and devastated by the event. It took an emotional toll on him that left him struggling with depression for many years. Yet he continued on in the calling God had given him and as a result impacted millions of people. He understood what it meant to face fear and great obstacles. Yet he chose to look past the fear and challenges and draw strength from the God he had entrusted his life to. He knew his God understood and cared. Out of his experience, he wrote the following:

> Our God's tender love for His servants makes Him concerned for the state of their inward feelings. He desires them to be of good courage. Some esteem it a small thing for a believer to be vexed with doubts and fears, but God thinks not so...our Master would not have us entangled with fears. He would have us without carefulness, without doubt, without cowardice. Our Master does not think so lightly of our unbelief as we do...The Christian man ought to be of a courageous spirit, in order that he may glorify the Lord by enduring trials in a heroic manner. If he be fearful and fainthearted, it will dishonour his God...Moreover, unless your courage is kept up Satan will be too much for you. Let your spirit

be joyful in God your Saviour, the joy of the Lord shall be your strength, and no fiend of hell shall make headway against you. But cowardice throws down the banner…The man who toils, rejoicing in his God, believing with all his heart, has success guaranteed. He who sows in hope shall reap in joy; therefore, dear reader, "be thou strong, and very courageous."[1]

Over and over in my life, God has asked me to do things that I was afraid of. Teaching, public speaking, getting my master's degree, and even writing this book! Each time, I initially reacted like Gideon, wondering if God had the right person. But every time that I faced my fears and came to the conclusion that I couldn't let fear win, God strengthened me and helped me to do what I didn't think I could do. God will do the same in your life if you don't let fear and insecurity win. Trust God and let the hero in you come out.

"The brave may not live forever, but the cautious do not live at all. For now you are traveling the road between who you think you are and who you can be."—Meg Cabot

8

STOP THE STINKIN' THINKIN'

My pastor has some humorous phrases he likes to use to make points memorable when he's preaching. One of those phrases is, "You gotta quit your stinkin' thinkin'!"

We all battle "stinkin' thinkin'" sometimes. Those negative, critical thoughts. Discouraging thoughts. Anxious and fearful thoughts. Sometimes our minds can take one negative thought and turn it into ten negative thoughts, and before you know it, a molehill has become a mountain. I imagine that process as a runaway mental train, barreling down the track until eventually everything derails. That's what negative, fear-based thinking can do—derail us mentally and emotionally, causing us to react and behave in ways that are opposite of what we'd really like to do.

Fear-based thinking produces anxiety, and anxiety very often goes hand-in-hand with depression. Fear and anxiety are strong feelings that tend to suck the life out of people. They are energy zappers. And the longer they control a person, the more hopeless the individual becomes, and eventually that hopelessness turns into depression.

Do you know what one of the most effective ways of treating anxiety and depression is? It's called Cognitive Behavioral Therapy, or CBT. Basically, it posits that if you correct the thoughts (cognition), you will change the behavior. People live what they believe. So much of fear, anxiety, and insecurity are all rooted in a person's beliefs. If a person thinks he is not intelligent, even if he has a high IQ, he will underperform. The anxiety that goes along with the belief hinders his performance. Or it will cause him to shy away from any intellectual challenges, for fear of failing or looking stupid.

I often tell my counseling clients that emotions can't determine if a thought or belief is true or rational. If you think depressing thoughts—e.g., I will never amount to anything; I can't ever seem to make friends; nothing ever changes for me—then you will feel sad or bad. You can't think negative thoughts and produce positive emotions. If you want to change how you feel, you have to change how you think. And when you change how you think and feel, you will change how you behave in life.

Long before psychologists figured this out, the Bible had it covered. The Bible is full of helpful instructions on taking control of your thought-life and focusing on things that are right, true, and positive.

The Bible even describes the mind as a type of spiritual battlefield, because the mind has so much influence over the person. Look at the following description of this battlefield in 2 Corinthians:

> For though we live in the world, we do not wage war as the world does. The weapons we fight with are not the weapons of the world. On the contrary, they have divine power to demolish strongholds. We demolish arguments and every pretension that sets itself up against the knowledge of God, and we take captive every thought to make it obedient to Christ (2 Corinthians 10:3–6).

When I read these verses and imagine a stronghold, I think of fortified cities in the Bible. They were surrounded by large walls, sometimes built into the side of mountains, and had high lookout towers, large gates, and iron bars. To capture the city, you had to get through its fortifications, which, as you can imagine, was no easy feat. These verses describe spiritual strongholds that are in the world. These strongholds are false and destructive beliefs that our enemy uses to keep people imprisoned—oppressed beliefs that are in complete opposition to the truth God wants them to know. God's truth sets people free from the things that would oppress and imprison them. Jesus said that when he said, "You will know the truth and the truth will set you free" (John 8:32).

God has given us spiritual weapons to take down the spiritual strongholds of lies and false beliefs. One of the spiritual weapons is the Word of God, the Bible. It holds the truths God wants us to believe. When we read and study the Bible, we fill our spiritual arsenal. This weapon of truth has divine power to demolish strongholds. God's truth has the power to demolish Satan's lies. We can take God's truth and demolish Satan's arguments, criticisms, condemnation—everything he uses against the knowledge of God. We fight the lies with the truth.

There is a second thing we can do in this battle of the mind. We can take every thought captive to make it obedient to Christ. In other words, we can decide to no longer let our minds run away with negative, stinkin' thinkin'. We can stop the mental train from running down the track.

We can decide to pay attention to what we are thinking and not allow ourselves to continue to dwell on and imagine worse and worse things. We can pause and evaluate our thoughts and ask ourselves, "Is this true according to what Christ would have me think?"

That is what it means to make your thoughts obedient to Christ. Evaluate your thoughts. What basis do you have for believing they are true?

Decide Whom You Will Listen To

Satan is called the Father of Lies. It is his mission to lie to people and deceive them in the hopes that he can destroy their lives and keep them from believing all the promises and good things God has for them.

One of the reasons this truly is a battle is because lies feel true. They are deceptive. And lies often have a little bit of truth mixed in to make them confusing or harder to discern as lies. Lies often start as tiny seeds of doubt. Satan began his quest to deceive Eve with the question, *Did God really say...?* And with a slight twist of the truth, he began planting doubt in Eve's mind.

Satan is subtle. He doesn't often come at us with blatant lies. He's underhanded. Often, there will be painful circumstances around false beliefs and lies we struggle with. For example, a child who has been sexually abused often believes he is at fault. That is not the least bit true, but Satan has a way of taking negative, painful experiences and attaching some of the most egregious lies to them: *I'm no good. People are going to reject me. I'm not worth loving. God doesn't love me or he wouldn't have let that happen.*

A lie can become a deeply held belief, a stronghold. Impenetrable, unshakeable, holding a person in bondage sometimes for one's whole life.

The devil also works through people in our lives. Sometimes his words come in the form of unwarranted criticism, harsh words, and outright lies about who we are, or through naysaying—words of opposition and pessimism, words that deflate hopes and crush dreams.

There is a sad account in the Bible of the power of fear and naysaying. God had promised his people, the Israelites, a wonderful land, flowing with milk and honey. He would bless their crops, their cattle, and their children. It would be a place of prosperity, health, and peace, as long as the Israelites lived in obedience to and trusted in the Lord. There were many people occupying the land who would have to be driven out, but God promised that his power would be with Israel and the Israelites would indeed be able to conquer the land. God had Moses send twelve spies into the land to survey it and bring back a report to the rest of the Israelites, in preparation of occupying it. Look at the account in Numbers 13:

> They came back to Moses and Aaron and the whole Israelite community at Kadesh in the Desert of Paran. There they reported to them and to the whole assembly and showed them the fruit of the land. They gave Moses this account: "We went into the land to which you sent us, and it does flow with milk and honey! Here is its fruit. But the people who live there are powerful, and the cities are fortified and very large." Then Caleb silenced the people before Moses and said, "We should go up and take possession of the land, for we can certainly do it." But the men who had gone up with him said, "We can't attack those people; they are stronger than we are." And they spread among the Israelites a bad report about the land they had explored. They said, "The land we explored devours those living in it. All the people we saw there are of great size…We seemed like grasshoppers in our own eyes, and we looked the same to them" (Num. 13:26–28, 30–33).

Look at the difference between the reports of the land based on either fear or faith. Ten of the spies let fear rule them and could only focus on how big the people looked. Even though God had promised he would help them defeat the occupants of Canaan, those ten refused to believe, focused on the negative, and were filled with fear. Two spies, Joshua and Caleb, were filled with faith.

Caleb's response was one of total confidence: "We should go up and take possession of the land, for *we can certainly do it*" (emphasis mine). Sadly, the ten negative spies continued spewing words of fear, doubt, and pessimism. Not only were their hearts deflated, but they influenced their fellow Israelites with fear-based thinking:

That night all the people of the community raised their voices and wept aloud. All the Israelites grumbled against Moses and Aaron, and the whole assembly said to them, "If only we had died in Egypt! Or in this desert! Why is the LORD bringing us to this land only to let us fall by the sword? Our wives and children will be taken as plunder. Wouldn't it be better for us to go back to Egypt?" And they said to each other, "We should choose a leader and go back to Egypt." Then Moses and Aaron fell facedown in front of the whole Israelite assembly gathered there. Joshua son of Nun and Caleb son of Jephunneh, who were among those who had explored the land, tore their clothes and said to the entire Israelite assembly, "The land we passed through and explored is exceedingly good. If the LORD is pleased with us, he will lead us into that land, a land flowing with milk and honey, and will give it to us. Only do not rebel against the LORD. And do not be afraid of the people of the land, because we will swallow them up. Their protection is gone, but the LORD is with us. Do not be afraid of them." (Num. 14:1–9)

The lies of the ten negative spies were so powerful that the Israelites not only began to doubt God's promise, but they actually believed God brought them to the land to destroy them and their children! Notice the progression of negative thinking, beginning with the thought that the people in the land were too big to fight and ending with "God is out for our destruction." Literally, the story begins with God giving his people a wonderful promise of how he would bless their lives and ends with the Israelites concluding that God's motivation was to destroy them and their children, and that being slaves in Egypt would be better!

That's the power of deception! And it begins with doubting the truth. Only those who trusted God and his character were convinced that God was going to deliver on his promise.

Satan's endgame in lying to us is to eventually lead us to the point of believing that God isn't for us, that God isn't really good, and that he is, in fact, the liar. Satan won't actually tell you God is lying to you; he will just attempt to get you to doubt God's promises and character.

There are a number of important lessons in this story. First, people will speak words of fear and doubt to you. You will have naysayers in your life. Satan wants you to believe the lies so you will stop trusting God. If you stop trusting God, you won't be able to experience all the wonderful things he has for your life. Second, you have to fight against the lies. Joshua, Caleb, Moses, and Aaron stood their ground. Vastly outnumbered and threatened with stoning, they were willing to keep their thoughts and lives obedient to God and stand on the truth.

When you are fighting lies and mental strongholds, at times it will feel like you are outnumbered. The lies might feel true. But stand your ground. Trust God. Keep your thoughts and life obedient to Christ.

"Resist the devil and he will flee from you" (James 4:7).

Eventually, you will receive the promises that the truth has offered you. All of the naysaying Israelites died in the wilderness because of their doubt. Only the believing spies, Joshua and Caleb, were allowed to enter the Promised Land and experience the blessings God had for them.

Don't let the lies, doubts, and fear of the enemy rob you of what God has for you. Christ has offered you a more abundant life, and your enemy doesn't want you to have it. Go take the promised land God has given you. Believe it, fight for it, and be blessed by it.

God Didn't Give You Fear and Insecurity

The Bible says, "For God has not given us a spirit of fear, but of power and of love and of a sound mind" (2 Tim. 1:7 NKJV).

God has not given us a spirit of fear or timidity. What is the opposite of fear and timidity? Peace, love, and confidence. Sound thinking. Those are the things God wants us to have. He doesn't want us to feel weak; he wants us to feel strong and confident. Faith-filled thinking doesn't comprise irrational, pie-in-the-sky hopes. It's based on rational, truth-filled beliefs. God is who he says he is, and the Bible says he cannot lie.

When we battle fear, anxiety, and insecurity, we need to grab our spiritual weapon of truth and start knocking down those lies that have been so strong in our lives. Lies that have made us feel weak, fearful, unloved, and insecure.

Instead of focusing on the stinkin' thinkin', fill your mind with faith-infusing thoughts.

"Finally, brothers, whatever is true, whatever is noble, whatever is right, whatever is pure, whatever is lovely, whatever is admirable—if anything is excellent or praiseworthy—think about such things" (Phil. 4:8).

Dwell on the truth. Let the truth rule in you. Spend time in the Word of God, memorizing, meditating, and obeying it. I often tell people, if you don't fill your mind with God's truth, the Holy Spirit has nothing to work with when you need his help in fighting false beliefs and knowing the truth!

The Holy Spirit is called the Spirit of Truth, the Counselor, the Comforter—one who is our constant companion, guide, teacher, and advocate. He reveals truth. The Bible also says that the sword (weapon) of the Spirit is the Word of God. Your weapon in spiritual warfare is the Word of God, your sword. As you apply and obey what you are taught, transformation and freedom happen!

That's what Romans 12:1–2 tell us: "Therefore, I urge you, brothers, in view of God's mercy, to offer your bodies as living sacrifices, holy and pleasing to God—this is your spiritual act of worship. Do not conform any longer to the pattern of this world, but be transformed by the renewing of your mind. Then you will be able to test and approve what God's will is—his good, pleasing and perfect will" (Rom. 12:1–2).

Romans 12:1–2 tells us that as we learn to live lives in alignment with God's truth, we will not only be transformed, permanently changed in the way we think, but we will also develop the ability to discern and be confident in what is the good, pleasing, and perfect will of God. We begin to build strongholds of truth in our lives, truths that are not easily knocked down!

The Eighteen-Inch Drop

I often hear people say that they believe Bible truths in their minds, but their hearts often struggle to believe. Perhaps you've heard the expression, "The truth needs to make the eighteen-inch drop from our minds to our hearts."

That is a very real dilemma for every believer. God says in Hebrews that those who would live in a covenant relationship with Jesus Christ would have his laws written not only in their minds, but also in their hearts: "This is the covenant that I will make with them after those days, says the LORD: I will put My laws into their hearts, and in their minds I will write them" (Heb. 10:16–17).

Why would that be necessary? Because our hearts contain our will, passions, and motivations. We live out of what our hearts believe. The Bible says that as a man thinks in his heart, so is he (Prov. 23:7 NKJV). We believe with our hearts, so our hearts are the seat of our faith (Rom. 10:9–10). Our mind is not. Our minds are the doorway for information (truth) to come in, but our hearts must embrace the truth and believe it.

The Holy Spirit works with our hearts to help us believe. He does that by giving us a revelation of the truth, an understanding of the truth from God's viewpoint. In Ephesians 1, Paul prayed that the believers would be given a spirit of wisdom and revelation to know God better. He asked God to open the eyes of their hearts: "I keep asking that the God of our Lord Jesus Christ, the glorious Father, may give you the Spirit of wisdom and revelation, so that you may know him better. I pray also that the eyes of your heart may be enlightened in order that you may know the hope to which he has called you, the riches of his glorious inheritance in the saints, and his incomparably great power for us who believe" (Eph. 1:17–20).

Have you ever thought about that? That your heart needs to "see" or "know" the truth about what God has for you? And it needs to come through the Holy Spirit giving you understanding and increasing your faith, which resides in your heart! That is what it means to receive revelation from God.

So how does revelation happen? It comes by spending time reading and meditating on the Word of God, but also spending time in the presence of God through prayer, worship, and sitting quietly in his presence, giving him your undivided attention. God can't speak if you aren't listening! Know that God wants to talk to you. He wants you to understand, not just have knowledge that doesn't really change you because you're struggling to believe it. Revelation from the Spirit of God makes the knowledge in your mind drop the eighteen inches!

We talked earlier how Satan tries to attack our minds with lies. He also tries to wound our hearts and rock our faith. He tests our hearts regarding the seeds of truth that have been planted there.

In the parable of the sower and seed, Jesus describes a heart (soil) that receives truth (seed) initially with great joy. He describes the soil of that heart as rocky, because the seed never takes root.

"The one who received the seed that fell on rocky places is the man who hears the word and at once received it with joy. But since he has no root, he lasts only a short time. When trouble or persecution comes because of the word, he quickly falls away" (Matt. 13:20–21).

The seed (truth) that is planted gets tested by persecution or trouble. Since the seed hasn't had a chance to take root, it dies. When it does, the person falls away or gets offended and stops believing. We can expect that every truth that God is trying to plant in our hearts will be tested. Circumstances will arise that may appear to be the opposite of what we believe based on the truth God is planting in us.

For example, let's say God is planting the truth in a person's heart that he is his provider and will be faithful to meet his needs according to his riches in glory. The person is excited and embraces that truth, but soon circumstances arise that begin to test his faith in that area. His car breaks down, a potential layoff is looming, and the furnace goes out. He prays and asks God for his help, but no money drops out of the sky. Now the testing has begun. Will the person let his faith grow? Will he stay determined to believe scripture, walk by faith, and keep trusting God to see him through? If he does, the seed takes root in his heart and his faith grows stronger. However, if he gets discouraged and disillusioned, he will give up, become offended at God, and potentially fall away.

Jesus explains in the parable of the sower and the seed how to have a heart that produces good spiritual fruit.

"But the seed on good soil stands for those with a noble and good heart, who hear the word, retain it, and by persevering produce a good crop" (Luke 8:15).

Listen Closely

First of all, we have to be willing to hear the word, or perhaps a better way of saying it is we have to listen to what we're told. We all know the difference between hearing something and actually listening. Listening requires attention. Sounds (e.g., words) can hit our auditory senses, but if we don't really give them attention, they don't really register. I think all parents understand this phenomenon when they tell their children what to do. When my son was young, I often needed him to repeat what I said to him to make sure he was actually listening. And before that happened, I made sure he was looking at me, giving me his attention.

Sometimes it can be hard to hear something God has told us because it's something we don't want to hear. When we don't like what God tells us, we reject it, or at the very least ignore it. We may know it's true and the right thing, but we just don't want to listen, and as a result, it never takes root in our heart, so we stay stuck in whatever area it was supposed to help us grow.

Not every seed of truth that God wants to plant in us will always be easy to receive. For example, it can be very hard to accept that you have to forgive everyone, no matter what a person's done or how often she's done it. Receiving that truth can be very, very difficult for some, and perhaps, depending on what they've suffered, that is very understandable. Taking up our cross and following Christ can be a hard word to receive. That's not always a pew-packing message! We as human beings don't often like to sacrifice. We'd prefer a comfortable life, and not every truth from God will make us comfortable. Every truth brings freedom and even joy at times, but not always comfort.

Have you ever gotten advice from someone that at first didn't sound appealing, but after you applied it and saw the beneficial results, you understood the wisdom of the advice? That will often be the case with God and his truth. There may be times that initially you don't see the wisdom of the advice. But knowing that he is a reliable, trustworthy source, you can take his advice and apply it.

Don't Be Wishy-Washy

That leads us to the next thing Jesus tells us to do to produce good spiritual fruit from his word: retain the word. Keep it. Hang on to it and don't let go. Don't be wishy-washy with the truth. James 1:8 says a double-minded man is unstable in all he does. Double-minded means to vacillate in opinion or purpose. The only thing that produces is instability.

The final thing that Jesus says we must do is to persevere in the truth. We talked earlier about the fact that we will be tested in our beliefs. That is a sure thing, so we must determine that we will persevere against all opposition. We live in a culture that often stands in direct opposition to the truths of God's Word. It isn't easy to stand for the truth. You will more than likely feel like a fish swimming upstream. However, God's truth has the power to bring transformation and abundant life like nothing this earth can offer. Believe that the reward is worth it. James 1 promises blessing for those who listen, retain, and obey the word of God:

> Do not merely listen to the word, and so deceive yourselves. Do what it says. Anyone who listens to the word but does not do what it says is like a man who looks at his face in a mirror and, after looking at himself, goes away and immediately forgets what he looks like. But the man who looks intently into the perfect law that gives freedom, and continues to do this, not forgetting what he has heard, but doing it—he will be blessed in what he does (James 1:22–25).

Satan is after your mind and your heart. Guard what you let into both of them. Fill them with things that will make you stronger, more confident, and more faith-filled. Love God with them and see what amazing things he has in store for you!

"Jesus replied: 'Love the Lord your God with all your heart and with all your soul and with all your mind'" (Matt. 22:37).

9

THE FIRST STEP IS THE SCARIEST

Life is full of firsts. In fact "firsts" are often very important to us. Ask any parent whose baby says his first word or takes his first step. Most of us can probably remember our first love (or perhaps first crush), regardless of whether it was good or bad. Firsts bring an excitement and anticipation of things to come.

We all know that first place is what everyone guns for in competition. No one hopes to take second place. After all, first place has all the status. Let's face it: Everyone secretly wishes to be chosen first in grade-school phys ed when teams are being created for kickball.

So what does this have to do with overcoming fear and living a life of faith? Everything. Every new venture of faith requires taking the first step, which is often the biggest and scariest. It's the first thing you do in spite of the fact that it may seem crazy, or if you're not certain that what you're doing is going to work out like you believe it will.

Take a look at the Biblical definition of faith found in Hebrews 11:1: "Now faith is being sure of what we hope for and certain of what we do not see" (Heb. 11:1).

That's a great picture of true faith—a complete assurance that what we are hoping for from God is going to happen. It's an unshakeable certainty based on complete trust that God will do what he says, no matter what. However, the reality is, few of us have faith that pure. Most of us have some mix of faith, fear, and doubt. Faith only becomes really strong and pure when it is exercised consistently—road tested.

Most of us have probably heard the analogy regarding faith and muscle. Only muscles that are worked out on a regular basis get stronger, and so it is with faith. However, as we all know, it's not that scary to work our muscles (OK, a few of us may have some gym phobias), but muscle-building is a normal, natural occurrence, proven by science. Faith, on the other hand, is all about the supernatural. You have to believe in the invisible, what your natural eyes don't see. It requires a great deal of trust in a God you can't see. That's why the first step is so critical when it comes to faith. It is the juncture at which we look fear and doubt directly in the face and decide we are going to go through with whatever it is God wants us to do.

The Bible has some practical examples of this first-step principle. Let's fast-forward a bit from our story where previously, the Israelites were filled with fear regarding taking their promised land, Canaan. The fearful generation that refused to believe God died out and their children were about to cross the Jordan into Canaan to begin driving out the inhabitants. Joshua was now their leader and had been given a new report about the people occupying Canaan. Their enemies became the ones filled with fear. Everyone knew God was with the Israelites, and they were filled with faith and ready to claim their blessing. Before that happened, though, God would have to do some miracles. The first was getting them across the Jordan River while it was in flood stage.

Look at how God solved the problem:

Joshua said to the Israelites, "Come here and listen to the words of the LORD your God. This is how you will know that the living God is among you and that he will certainly drive out before you the Canaanites, Hittites, Hivites, Perizzites, Girgashites, Amorites and Jebusites. See, the ark of the covenant of the Lord of all the earth will go into the Jordan ahead of you. Now then, choose twelve men from the tribes of Israel, one from each tribe. And as soon as the priests who carry the ark of the LORD—the Lord of all the earth—set foot in the Jordan, its waters flowing downstream will be cut off and stand up in a heap." So when the people broke camp to cross the Jordan, the priests carrying the Ark of the Covenant went ahead of them. Now the Jordan is at flood stage all during harvest. Yet as soon as the priests who carried the ark reached the Jordan and their feet touched the water's edge, the water from upstream stopped flowing. It piled up in a heap a great distance away, at a town called Adam in the vicinity of Zarethan, while the water flowing down to the Sea of the Arabah (the Salt Sea) was completely cut off. So the people crossed over opposite Jericho. The priests who carried the ark of the covenant of the LORD stood firm on dry ground in the middle of the Jordan, while all Israel passed by until the whole nation had completed the crossing on dry ground" (Josh. 3:9–17).

This wasn't the first time God parted a large body of water, and the Israelites knew it. However, God was going to do it a little differently than the Red Sea parting (no putting God in a box!). The priests carrying the Ark of the Covenant actually had to step into the water while it was at flood stage. They had to take a step first before the miracle happened. It wasn't Joshua holding a rod up and all of a sudden the waters parted. God asked his people to take a step of faith. As a result, God did something supernatural in response to their faith. God always responds to obedient faith, guaranteed. As their feet touched the water's edge, the water stopped flowing and piled up in a giant heap far away. God not only cleared a very wide path so all the Israelites could cross as quickly as possible, but they didn't even get their sandals muddy!

Notice something important in this story that holds true for any journey from fear to faith: God led the way. Joshua assured the people that the Ark of the Covenant, the place where the Lord of all the earth dwelt, was going to go ahead of the people. Not only did God go ahead of the Israelites, but his presence also stayed in the middle of the Jordan so that every Israelite was able to pass by and know that he was right there with them.

When God asks you to do anything in faith, you can be assured that he will go ahead of you to lead the way. Not only will God respond supernaturally to your first step of faith, but he will continue to stay with you every step of the way. Whatever your Jordan journey is, God will be right in the middle of it with you.

It Takes Trust

At the core of being able to take steps of faith is the ability to trust. Trust isn't always an easy thing, especially if people have let us down, hurt us, lied to us, or in any way acted without integrity. I think I can safely say that all of us have experienced having our trust broken.

It would seem that within our culture, there is an increasing lack of integrity within people's lifestyles, causing an even-greater breakdown of trust.

An interesting study came out of Penn State University, led by Dr. Nancy Darling, on the extent of teen dishonesty or lying. Dr. Darling enlisted the help of a dozen undergraduate students to help interview local high school students. Each student was given a deck of thirty-six cards, each card containing a topic teens tend to lie to their parents about. Of all the students, 98 percent felt that honesty and trust were critical in relationships, and, depending on their ages, 96 to 98 percent believed it is morally wrong to lie.

Each student went through the deck and identified which topics they lied to their parents about and why. It was eye-opening to the students to discover just how much they lie to their parents and how many family rules they break. The study revealed that 98 percent admitted to lying, and of the thirty-six topics, the average number of things lied about was twelve. The topics included lying about dating, how their allowance was spent, whether there were chaperones at parties, drug and alcohol use, what movie they went to and with whom, if they were riding in a car with a drunk friend driving, what they did with their time when their parents weren't at home, and whether they were hanging out with inappropriate friends. The statistics were consistent with surveys of teens across the United States.

So how do 98 percent of teens who believe trust and honesty are essential in relationships become the 98 percent of teens who lie? According to the study, it is because their parents teach them to! They learn to lie from their parents in everyday situations, such as telling the telemarketer they are just a guest in the home, or telling Aunt Betty how much they loved the gift she made, even though they hated it. White lies are indirectly communicated to the children as ways of being socially polite. The message children receive is that honesty can cause conflict, so it's better to tell a white lie and keep things peaceful.

You can imagine what that progresses to. Children learn that lying protects them from things getting uncomfortable. There is a seemingly good reward for the white lies. Interestingly, although the children could tell the difference between a white lie meant to be "polite" and a lie about their behavior, the freedom to tell white lies laid the groundwork for other types of lying. Dishonesty and insincerity is a result of lying, no matter what color you think the lie is. Sadly, the parents in the study just couldn't seem to understand that white lies are still lies and lead to more lying. When asked to keep a record of their lies, the adults lied an average of once in every five social interactions, which equated to at least one lie per day.

If people on average are lying at least once a day, it is no wonder so many people in our culture struggle to trust.

Untrustworthy Christians?

In the book *Unchristian*, author David Kinnaman and the Barna Group did extensive research into the perceptions of people age sixteen to twenty-nine (called Mosaics and Busters) regarding Christians and Christianity. The perceptions are not flattering. One significant perception is that Christians are hypocritical. That may not sound like anything new, but there is something different with this generation in regard to how the concept of hypocrisy affects them. According to the research, they are not greatly bothered by it and, in fact, have come to expect it in everyone, not just Christians. Kinnaman writes:

Mosaics and Busters are not bothered by the image as much as you might think. They have learned not to care. In large part this is because they have come to the conclusion that people cannot be counted on, that one should expect to be disappointed. I was surprised how frequently young outsiders [of Christianity] simply blew off the hypocrisy issue. One example: "Yeah, everyone is hypocritical at some point. It is not a general failing of Christianity that its practitioners are prone to the same faults as the rest of us." Or this: "Hypocrisy is a common occurrence in most people's lives. It happens. Get over it."[1]

People have become jaded and no longer balk at inconsistencies and incongruence between words and actions. It is almost as though we expect that people will lie and not do what they say. Even more alarming is the large gap between what born-again Christians in the United States claim they believe and how they actually live. Kinnaman describes this disparity as follows:

In virtually every study we conduct, representing thousands of interviews every year, born-again Christians fail to display much attitudinal or behavioral evidence of transformed lives. For instance, based on a study released in 2007, we found that most of the lifestyle activities of born-again Christians were statistically equivalent to those of non-born-agains. When asked to identify their activities over the last thirty days, born-again believers were just as likely to bet or gamble, to visit a pornographic website, to take something that didn't belong to them, to consult a medium or psychic, to physically fight or abuse someone, to have consumed enough alcohol to be considered legally drunk, to have used an illegal, nonprescription drug, to have said something to someone that is not true, to have gotten back at someone for something he or she did, and to have said mean things behind another person's back.

Imagine people's perception of Christ based on how Christians' lives represent him. If Christians, who are supposed to be people who are honest, ethical, and morally trustworthy, are really not any of those things, why should they be trusted, and why would God be any more trustworthy?

Trust in many ways is a learned trait. We trust when we experience situations in life that help us know someone or something can be trusted. So many people so rarely experience trustworthy people and situations in life that they hardly even understand the concept of trust. So how in the world do they trust a God that they can't see? It will require a supernatural encounter with God that reveals to them his trustworthy nature. In essence, God needs to reveal himself and prove himself. He is willing to do that, but it's a great chasm God often has to bridge because we humans (especially Christians) have dropped the ball in a big way.

Some people reading this may feel compelled to argue that we Christians are not perfect, just forgiven. I wholeheartedly agree. However, that doesn't absolve us of our responsibility to live a life worthy of our Christian calling and at least make a diligent attempt at obeying the moral principles of God's Word. The apostle Paul prayed for the early Christians that they would not only know the Lord's will, but live it:

> For this reason, since the day we heard about you, we have not stopped praying for you and asking God to fill you with the knowledge of his will through all spiritual wisdom and understanding. And we pray this in order that you may live a life worthy of the Lord and may please him in every way: bearing fruit in every good work, growing in the knowledge of God, being strengthened with all power according to his glorious might so that you may have great endurance and patience, and joyfully giving thanks to the Father, who has qualified you to share in the inheritance of the saints in the kingdom of light. For he has rescued us from the dominion of darkness and brought us into the kingdom of the Son he loves, in whom we have redemption, the forgiveness of sins (Col. 1:9–14).

We are Christ's ambassadors to this world, called to be salt and light. If we still live in darkness as Christians, we don't represent Christ, period.

One of the fruits of the Spirit is faithfulness. Some Bibles translate it as "faith," but faithfulness is actually a more descriptive word. It implies dependability—fidelity, loyalty, and obedience. Faith and faithfulness are meant to be an expression of our deepest convictions. That expression should be manifested in our lives.

Jesus Christ became the outward manifestation of the faithful convictions of God. Jesus showed us what matters to God and that God would be absolutely unwavering in fulfilling what he said he'd do. Over the course of thousands of years, there were many prophecies foretelling the coming of Jesus Christ for the express purpose of revealing God to mankind and providing hope and salvation to everyone who would believe. Jesus Christ fulfilled every prophecy to the letter. And some of those prophecies were painful. He knew he would be beaten, spit on, scorned, and doubted by the very ones he would give his life for. Jesus willingly went through the worst suffering any human could endure because he and the Father intended to keep their word and do what they said they would do.

> Now when people take an oath, they call on someone greater than themselves to hold them to it. And without any question that oath is binding. God also bound himself with an oath, so that those who received the promise could be perfectly sure that he would never change his mind. So God has given both his promise and his oath. These two things are unchangeable because it is *impossible for God to lie*. Therefore, we who have fled to him for refuge can have great confidence as we hold to the hope that lies before us. This hope is a strong and trustworthy anchor for our souls." (Heb. 6:16–19 NLT, emphasis mine)

God cannot and does not lie. He is fully trustworthy. We give him opportunities to prove that to us by taking him at His word. We give Him the opportunity to prove himself. As he does, our trust builds. Everyone can learn to trust, because there is a true source of trustworthiness to learn from, Jesus Christ. He is the same yesterday, today, and forever. Man will let us down. Parents, friends, coworkers, fellow Christians will let us down. Man is not perfect. But God is. That's why the Israelites would step into the Jordan River while it was at flood stage. A ludicrous act unless the God who is faithful and true tells you to do it, because he will part the river if you do.

God's trustworthiness is the basis for our ability to take any first step of faith—or any step for that matter! And as I mentioned earlier, God does things to build our faith and trust in him. Before the Israelites had to cross the Jordan, they had a long history of God showing up in powerful ways to kick-start their trust in him. As they journeyed through the wilderness (a result of their *lack* of faith), God supplied a cloud by day and fire by night to lead and protect them. He never let their shoes wear out.

Food and water were always provided when they needed it (or when they asked for it). God would give them smaller tests to build their faith, obedience, and trust. For example, God gave them manna each day to supply their needs, but he made them do exactly what he told them to do when they went out to gather it. They could not collect too little or too much. If they gathered too much, it would rot. Too little, and they went hungry. He taught them a key lesson—you can't have real faith without obedience. Obedience is the evidence of trust.

<u>Love and Trust Are Not the Same</u>

Sometimes we can confuse the fact that love and trust are not the same thing. In other words, we can know someone loves us but still not completely trust him. Love can produce trust, but one can know she is loved without trusting fully the one who loves her.

When my son Caleb was going into second grade, he started a new school and was absolutely terrified. He didn't like change. And he certainly didn't like the unknown. As I walked him to his new classroom, he immediately flung his little arms around my neck with a vise grip and began to wail uncontrollably, begging me not to leave him there. As much as Caleb knew that I loved him, in that moment, he didn't trust me that I wasn't leaving him in a jungle with wild animals. Because he was young and had much more maturing to do, he didn't know how to process that he was safe. I had to let him feel uncomfortable until he discovered that everything was actually OK. It was a good situation, not a bad, scary one.

That's why many Christians may know God loves them but still struggle to take steps of faith that require them to trust him. We are afraid of the unknown. Over the years, I have had many, many experiences of God asking me to do something that made me want to throw my arms around him and beg him not to make me do it. It has always been those times of God asking me to do something out of my comfort zone, out of the realm of the familiar into the unknown. And like my son, I have been terrified, in spite of the fact that each time I could have told you that God loved me and always had my best interest at heart. While love and trust are not the same thing, the unconditional love of God also includes his trustworthiness and faithfulness. They are attributes of his love. Having a broader, deeper revelation of who God is and how long, deep, and wide his love is will inevitably produce a greater trust. One who loves so perfectly cannot be anything but trustworthy. It is the maturing of our perspective of God that causes us to live in greater trust. Remember how much "smarter" your parents seemed after you became an adult compared to what you thought as a teenager? It's the maturing of our perspectives.

Trusting Beyond the First Step

In chapter 4, I briefly mentioned a story found in Matthew 14:22–33, where the apostle Peter takes a big step of faith (literally) and walks on water. In the story, Jesus and his disciples had been ministering to crowds of people for the whole day. Jesus, ready to spend some time alone in prayer, sent his disciples on ahead of him by boat as he retreated to a mountainside. As evening came, the winds picked up and the disciples began a long night of battling high winds and turbulent waters. After struggling into the wee hours of the morning, probably somewhere around 3:00 a.m., Jesus walked out on the water to the disciples. As he approached them, the disciples finally noticed Jesus and were scared out of their minds, thinking he was a ghost. However, Jesus spoke to them and assured them it was him. He told them to take courage. They no longer needed to be afraid. He was there with them.

That alone makes for an interesting story, but that's not the end of it. Peter, who was normally a bit impulsive, asked Jesus to bid him to come to him on the water. Notice Peter didn't ask Jesus if he could *swim* to him; he asked if he could come to him *on the water*. Apparently Peter had this crazy notion that if Jesus walked on water and Jesus wanted Peter to walk on water, then Peter himself *could* actually walk on water! All he needed was for Jesus to say the word. All right, Peter. Come. It was in that moment that Peter had a big decision to make. He had to take the first step. He had to climb over the side of the boat and put his foot down...on water. Peter would never know if the water would support him until he actually stepped on it. Peter didn't flop over the side of the boat like a search-and-rescue diver; he just stepped out of the boat and began to walk.

Notice what *didn't* happen. At that particular point, the wind *didn't* die down and the waves *didn't* calm. Peter had to take that first step when the waters were turbulent and the wind was gusting. That certainly raised the faith stakes a bit. If Jesus had calmed the wind and waters first and this water-walking venture didn't work, Peter would just end up taking a chilly dip in the lake. As a seasoned fisherman, he'd probably taken quite a few lake swims in his day. But not when winds were gusting and waves were crashing. That's the time you stay in the boat.

So taking that first step out of the boat was a huge step...of faith. Either Jesus would do something supernatural for Peter, or that boy was going down! Peter had to weigh his options at that point. Every rational argument, every "what if" must have flashed through his mind in those first thirty seconds. But Peter chose to believe that if Jesus told him to come to him on the water, then that's exactly what he could do. No more arguments. So he took that all-important first step. And his faith was rewarded with an experience that was nothing less than miraculous. Peter walked on water. And every step after that was miraculous, each one sustained by the power of God. All twenty supernatural steps (or whatever the number) required the first step.

People have often been critical of Peter in this story, saying he was being impulsive. Typical Peter. I have to disagree. I believe this account of Peter actually displayed Peter's growth and maturity. He asked Jesus to help him do what he saw Jesus doing. He got Jesus's permission; he didn't just jump out of the boat on impulse. Peter showed a trust in Christ that the eleven other boat warmers didn't. They apparently didn't even entertain the thought that if Jesus could walk on water, perhaps they could, too, by the power of God. In some ways, the greatest step Peter took was the one where he asked Jesus if he could do something that required supernatural power! As we continue to grow in our faith and trust God more, we can actually begin to ask him for opportunities to trust him to do the supernatural through us!

After Peter had taken a few steps, he did what probably many of us would do: He began to notice the difficult circumstances around him. A storm was raging, gusty winds and waves were crashing all around. He took his eyes off of Christ, and as soon as that happened, his faith melted and fear arose. And he began to sink. But that's not the end of the story. Jesus called Peter on his moment of doubt, but Jesus also did something else. He went to Peter, grabbed him, and helped him *walk* back the rest of the way to the boat. The miracle didn't end with Peter's momentary lack of faith. It wasn't a total showstopper.

Sometimes we take the first step of faith, then several more beyond it. But then opposition comes. Finances fall through, relationships turn sour, critics speak, or time passes without significant results. And we begin to doubt. We take our eyes off of Jesus, we stop looking to him to keep us going, and we begin to sink into doubt.

Thankfully, Jesus doesn't leave us there. Peter learned an all-important lesson about faith. When we fail, Jesus is there to pick us up again. Not only does he pick us up, he enables us to move forward supernaturally again. He can help us continue to move toward the goal that he originally called us to. We may have moments of fear in the middle of our journey of faith, but God doesn't abandon us at that moment. He lovingly corrects us, takes us by the hand, and guides us forward again. He helps us keep trusting him.

Often in life, when *we* fail people or let them down, we expect that they will abandon or reject us. We may feel that way about God. But Jesus proves to us in this story that the complete opposite happens. He meets us right where we failed and strengthens us to finish what we started. The water-walking lesson Peter learned about trusting Jesus, combined with many other lessons, would eventually cause Peter to become a spiritual pillar of the early church. Peter would one day trust Christ so much that at his own martyrdom, he would request to be crucified upside-down because he felt unworthy to be crucified in the same way that his Lord and Savior, Jesus Christ, was.

Notice what happens as Jesus and Peter get back into the boat: "And when they climbed into the boat, the wind died down. Then those who were in the boat worshiped him, saying, 'Truly you are the Son of God'" (Matt. 14:32–33).

After Jesus and Peter climbed into the boat, the wind died down and everyone in the boat recognized the majesty and greatness of Jesus and felt compelled to worship him. Christ's influence on them didn't include a sense of judgment and shame for not getting out of the boat with Peter. Whatever Jesus did as he interacted with those twelve men, it caused them to want to worship him.

Our attempts to take steps of faith and to trust God don't ever draw condemnation from Christ. He's pleased, even if we are not 100 percent successful. We receive grace and mercy and more power. The result is that we feel compelled to worship him even more.

Go ahead. Take the first step. Jesus is calling you, and he is with you and will be every step of the way.

10

STOP FEARING FEAR

"The only thing we have to fear is fear itself."

—Franklin D. Roosevelt

I think it's safe to assume that none of us like the feeling of fear, particularly when we feel threatened or in danger. People who regularly struggle with fear and anxiety can develop the habit of avoiding or escaping from situations that cause fear. When I was in my early twenties, I had been offered several different opportunities to take on greater leadership roles and do public speaking. I was so scared at the prospect of having to do more speaking that I found any excuse I could think of to avoid taking the new roles. I would use sickness as an out. The slightest twinge of any symptom would qualify as an out. I'm not thrilled to admit it, but I did it. I was that scared.

Over and over, I experienced the flood of relief that came when I knew I didn't have to speak. But I also experienced something else: increased fear later. Studies have shown that avoidance or escape actually leads to stronger fear because it reinforces the catastrophic thinking that fear tends to produce. Most of the time when people face their fears and push through them, they discover that what they feared didn't actually happen or at least things didn't turn out nearly as bad as they imagined. That is an important learning opportunity, but it is only attained by doing the thing you fear. Avoiding fearful situations also diminishes self-confidence. It may feel good in the moment, but long-term avoidance only causes people to feel even more insecure and inadequate. It becomes a vicious fear-avoidance cycle that leaves people trapped.

People who have made a mess of their finances will often avoid taking an in-depth inventory of their financial condition because they are too afraid of what they will see. What is the result of the avoidance? More bad money management and debt. Overweight people avoid stepping on the scale because they fear seeing how much they really weigh. The result? They go from being thirty pounds overweight to fifty pounds. Parents who battle fear of something bad happening to their children spend excessive amounts of energy and time trying to control every little situation in their child's life. However, something inevitably happens to the child that is difficult and the parents become weighed down with a sense of guilt and failure, even though they really had no power to prevent the difficulty.

Research has proven that the fear-avoidance cycle has a significantly negative effect on the quality of life, but that fear can be mastered when it is no longer avoided.

The only way to win the battle of fear is to face it. Psychology has a technique it uses to help facilitate that. It's called exposure therapy. There is no other way to learn that something is not really as bad as you think until you expose yourself to it. The technique actually involves exposure to things that a person is only mildly afraid of to facilitate a sense of mastery. The increase in exposure is gradual, but long enough so that the person learns a new response besides fear. Psychiatrist Karl Menninger said, "Fears are educated into us, and can, if we wish, be educated out."

Sometimes the learning involves recognizing irrational or untrue beliefs. In regard to my fear of public speaking, the more I spoke and got positive feedback, the more I was able to fight the untrue fears I had about how people were going to respond to my speaking. I shared earlier that there were many anxiety-producing thoughts I battled in relationship to speaking, but the only way I could deal with them was to speak!

As Dale Carnegie said, "Inaction breeds doubt and fear. Action breeds confidence and courage. If you want to conquer fear, do not sit home and think about it. Go out and get busy."

Believe it or not, you can stop fearing fear. Fear can be changed by not fearing it. In other words, we all have to develop a certain tolerance for the feeling of fear so that we are willing to face it long enough for it to lose its grip on us.

Dr. Kevin Arnold, director of the Center for Cognitive and Behavioral Therapy in Columbus, Ohio, wrote: "When we adopt a belief that we can tolerate being afraid, and take on the role of experimenter in our own lives, regaining the fullness and joy of living is possible. We become happier, less controlling, and more effective folks through acceptance of fear."

"Avoiding danger is no safer in the long run than outright exposure. The fearful are caught as often as the bold."—Helen Keller

Doing Hard Things

I'm sure you've heard the expression, "Whatever doesn't kill you makes you stronger." In many cases, that statement is true, provided we're willing to be made stronger. Sometimes fear arises over the anticipation of doing difficult things. Selling everything you have to do missions work in Africa is a hard thing. Adopting an at-risk youth into your family is a hard thing. Raising children in a world full of drugs, alcohol, and violent crime is a hard thing. So is dealing with cancer or facing a layoff in a down economy.

The anticipation of facing hard things can generate fear in us, and God knows it and addresses it in the Bible. There's a powerful example in Deuteronomy in which Joshua had a very daunting task ahead of him and God spoke through Moses to encourage Joshua to not let fear rule. Joshua was about to take over Moses's position of leading the Israelites into the land of Canaan. Look at what Moses told Joshua and the Israelites:

> Then Moses went out and spoke these words to all Israel: "I am now a hundred and twenty years old and I am no longer able to lead you. The LORD has said to me, 'You shall not cross the Jordan.' The LORD your God himself will cross over ahead of you. He will destroy these nations before you, and you will take possession of their land. Joshua also will cross over ahead of you, as the LORD said. And the LORD will do to them what he did to Sihon and Og, the kings of the Amorites, whom he destroyed along with their land. The LORD will deliver them to you, and you must do to them all that I have commanded you. Be strong and courageous. Do not be afraid or terrified because of them, for the LORD your God goes with you; he will never leave you nor forsake you." Then Moses summoned Joshua and said to him in the presence of all Israel, "Be strong and courageous, for you must go with this people into the land that the LORD swore to their forefathers to give them, and you must divide it among them as their inheritance. The LORD himself goes before you and will be with you; he will never leave you nor forsake you. Do not be afraid; do not be discouraged." (Deut. 31:1–8)

Remember, Joshua and Caleb were the only spies of the twelve sent that came back with an encouraging report of faith after spying out the land of Canaan. They believed that the land was good in spite of the size of the enemies who lived there, and they fully believed God would help them conquer the land. Joshua was a man of great faith, but now, not only would he be participating in many battles to drive the enemies out of their land, he would also take Moses's leadership role over the whole nation of Israel.

Joshua's job description and responsibility just increased a hundred times! Even men and women of great faith, when faced with large, daunting tasks, can feel twinges of fear and angst. Not only that, but it was inevitable that frustrating and discouraging things would happen during his tenure as leader of Israel. After all, Moses wanted to turn in his resignation more than once after dealing with the crazy problems that happened with the Israelites. Not many CEOs get threatened with stoning by their subordinates! Joshua was going to have his hands full. God understood what Joshua would need.

So Moses, under the leading of the Lord, told Joshua, "Be strong and courageous...do not be afraid; do not be discouraged." What they were about to do was not going to be easy. It would require great faith and endurance. When Moses died, God again spoke to Joshua, this time directly:

After the death of Moses the servant of the LORD, the LORD said to Joshua son of Nun, Moses' aide: "Moses my servant is dead. Now then, you and all these people, get ready to cross the Jordan River into the land I am about to give to them—to the Israelites. I will give you every place where you set your foot, as I promised Moses. Your territory will extend from the desert to Lebanon, and from the great river, the Euphrates—all the Hittite country—to the Great Sea on the west. No one will be able to stand up against you all the days of your life. As I was with Moses, so I will be with you; I will never leave you nor forsake you. Be strong and courageous, because you will lead these people to inherit the land I swore to their forefathers to give them. Be strong and very courageous. Be careful to obey all the law my servant Moses gave you; do not turn from it to the right or to the left, that you may be successful wherever you go. Do not let this Book of the Law depart from your mouth; meditate on it day and night, so that you may be careful to do everything written in it. Then you will be prosperous and successful. Have I not commanded you? Be strong and courageous.

Do not be terrified; do not be discouraged, for the LORD your God
will be with you wherever you go." (Josh. 1:1–9)

Courage in the face of fearful tasks. Sometimes we have to do good
things—right things—that are not easy. The right path is often not the
easy path. It takes courage. It takes the ability to endure and not get discouraged when the odds seem stacked against you. It means you have to
keep your eyes fixed on Jesus so that the winds and the waves crashing
around you don't cause you to be afraid. That is the reality of living a life
of faith. No one said it would be easy, not even God. When Jesus was preparing for his departure back to heaven, he encouraged his disciples with
these words: "In this world you will have trouble. But take heart! I have
overcome the world" (John 16:33).

The word in the Greek that is translated "trouble" is also translated as
"anguish," "burdened," "persecution," and "tribulation."

So let me cheer you up with my paraphrased version of John 16:33: "In
this world that you live in, you are going to be burdened, persecuted, and
will experience anguish and tribulation. These things may cause you to be
afraid, but be courageous, because I, Jesus, already experienced it all and
overcome it. I will never leave you nor forsake you, and I will give you the
power to be victorious and overcome all of it, too."

I was recently talking to a client who is a self-professed control freak.
The reason she controls so much is that she's afraid of things going wrong
and wants to do everything in her power to prevent it. The reality is that
none of us can prevent every negative thing from happening. Too much of
life is out of our control. So trying to control what you can't control only
leads to more anxiety and more control. Jesus has an answer for the fear
of things going wrong: be an overcomer, not a control freak. Jesus tells
us we can't prevent trouble from happening (you *will* have trouble), but we
can overcome it.

The type of work I do as a counselor often requires that I give my clients hard things to do if they want to find healing in their lives. Change is hard work. If it was easy, we'd all do it as quickly as possible so we could be happy as soon as possible. Everything worthwhile in life requires hard work and sacrifice. We want things to be so easy. We love to take the path of least resistance sometimes, but sadly that path only leads us to the harder life. We may hate where we are, but it doesn't require anything extra from us, so we're willing to stay unhappy rather than do the hard work to make the change for the better. We can't fear doing hard things, or we'll never move forward in life.

I opened this chapter with a quote from Franklin D. Roosevelt: "The only thing we have to fear is fear itself." It is from his first inaugural address on March 4, 1933. What I found interesting about this was at that time, Franklin Roosevelt was taking the helm as president during the Great Depression, the longest, most widespread depression in the twentieth century. The effect was devastating to countries throughout the world. International trade dropped by more than 50 percent, and unemployment in the United States increased to 25 percent (current unemployment rates in the United States as of May 2015 are at 5.5 percent). Every area of industry was affected, and in some countries, the negative effects lasted until the end of World War II. In addition, a severe drought occurred in the mid-1930s in the heartland of the United States. As a whole, the world economy hit bottom in 1933. These were the conditions President Roosevelt found himself in as he was addressing the United States in his inaugural speech. No doubt the climate in the United States contained much fear. With this in mind, here is a portion of that famed speech:

> I am certain that my fellow Americans expect that on my induction into the Presidency I will address them with a candor and a decision which the present situation of our people impel. This is preeminently the time to speak the truth, the whole truth, frankly and boldly. Nor need we shrink from honestly facing conditions in our country today. This great Nation will endure as it has endured,

will revive and will prosper. So, first of all, let me assert my firm belief that the only thing we have to fear is fear itself—nameless, unreasoning, unjustified terror which paralyzes needed efforts to convert retreat into advance. In every dark hour of our national life a leadership of frankness and vigor has met with that understanding and support of the people themselves which is essential to victory.[1]

He boldly and succinctly addresses the heart of the matter of facing hard things that would cause us to shrink back; the only thing we have to fear is fear itself, because fear—or terror, as he puts it—paralyzes efforts to convert retreat into advance. When we refuse to let fear paralyze us, we are mobilized into action and doors of opportunity begin to open. Opportunities for solutions, for new experiences, and for personal growth and freedom.

I love this quote by Eleanor Roosevelt: "The purpose of life is to live it, to taste experience to the utmost, to reach out eagerly and without fear for newer and richer experience."

Franklin Roosevelt's wife, Eleanor, was no stranger to hardship. Prior to being the First Lady during the tumultuous time of the Great Depression, she lost both her parents and her brother at a very young age. She also persevered through her husband's affair in 1918 and his paralysis resulting from polio. She had a significant role in politics and human rights activities. Gallup named her one of the most widely admired people of the twentieth century. She was a woman who faced many difficult and fear-inducing situations. Yet she was a woman who knew what it meant to be strong and courageous. If there was a person who knew what it took to conquer fear, it was her.

"You gain strength, courage and confidence by every experience in which you really stop to look fear in the face," she once said. "You are able to say to yourself, 'I have lived through this horror. I can take the next thing that comes along.' You must do the thing you think you cannot do."

Not long ago someone told me about a book with some unique insights on dealing with change and the unknown. Spencer Johnson's book *Who Moved My Cheese?* became an international best seller. It's a simple parable of four characters, two mice and two "little people," who go on a quest in a maze to find cheese, which represents those things in life that make people happy and bring fulfillment. There is a section in the story that talks about getting beyond fear. One of the little people, named Haw, is contemplating what he needs to do now that his cheese, in his current place, has run out. He knows he must go back into the maze, the unknown, and try once again to find cheese, and he's afraid. But he asks himself this question, "What would you do if you weren't afraid?"

Let me ask you the same question: "What would you do if you weren't afraid?"

Go ahead and do the thing you think you cannot do.

"Have I not commanded you? Be strong and courageous. Do not be terrified; do not be discouraged, for the Lord your God will be with you wherever you go" (Josh. 1:9).

11

WHAT EXACTLY IS THE FEAR OF GOD?

If you were to survey a large group of people and ask them how they would describe the God of the Bible (if in fact they believed that there is a God), you would most likely get answers that varied from a "hellfire and brimstone" God to a God of love who would never send anyone to hell. He might be described as the God who has a list of rules he'd like all of us to keep, and in general, if you do a pretty good job of keeping them, he'll be happy with you and you'll get to go to heaven. On the other hand, he might be considered the God who can't possibly expect anyone to live by what some consider to be the antiquated moral standards of the Bible, so for some, he's the God of moral relativism. Each person gets to decide for himself what is right regarding his relationship with God.

With so many different opinions about the God of the Bible, you'd think he has multiple personality disorder.

Now in all fairness to us mere mortals trying to interpret the Bible, it can be a bit of a challenge to understand a God who expresses himself in hyperbole, metaphor, symbolism, poetry, and paradox.

Jesus would often say things that no doubt made folks scratch their heads, such as "the first shall be last," "you have to die to live," and "in order to be great, you have to be a servant." Then there is also the more straightforward stuff, like trying to understand the historical context of a verse. For example, when is the last time someone paid you in drachmas?

From the beginning of creation, God has endeavored to reveal himself to humankind using various means and methods. If you think back to the Garden of Eden, things actually started out pretty clear and straightforward. There was open communication between God and Adam and Eve. God was quite excited and pleased with his creation and fully enjoyed the possibility of having a loving relationship with those he created in his image. They would walk and talk together in the cool of the garden. God had very clearly communicated what he expected of them. He would love them and provide for them, and they would respect him and honor him as God.

Something, however, enters into the picture that changes everything. Lies. False distortions about who God is and what he really thinks. Satan shows up to deceive Adam and Eve about their God, because Satan has a vendetta against God. God's people take the bait and believe the lies, and from that point on, everything changes. They have greatly disrespected God and have to deal with the consequences. Fear enters the picture. They had never been afraid of God before this, but they had also never dishonored or disobeyed him. Sin and shame enter their hearts as a result of choosing to dishonor and disrespect his authority. Where sin and shame exist, fear exists—fear of consequences.

Think for a moment what happens as you're cruising down the road and you see a police car. You immediately glance at your speedometer and your heart starts pounding if you are speeding. Why do you suddenly get nervous? Because you know if you're breaking the law, there will be consequences—in this case, a speeding ticket. However, if you are fully aware that you are not speeding, more than likely you won't be nervous when you see the police, because you have nothing to fear.

Here is where we begin our exploration of what the fear of God is. Up to this point, we've looked at the many ways God tries to set people *free* from fear, and now we have to reconcile that with the fact that God desires that we fear him. In fact, the Bible teaches in Psalm 111 that the fear of the Lord is the beginning of wisdom: "The fear of the LORD is the beginning of wisdom; all who follow his precepts have good understanding" (Ps. 111:10).

Why? Well, let's go back to the examples of Adam and Eve, and you and the police officer. Both imply that there are relationships in life that deserve respect and honor. When respect and honor are shown, things are good. There is peace. And in the case with God and his children, a relationship of unconditional love exists. That means love always exists, even in the case of disobedience. But there will be correction. And depending on how bad the behavior is, the correction may be unpleasant. But the relationships are not meant to be fear based, but respect based. The respect produces fear in the case of rebellion against what is right. This relationship is explained in Hebrews 12:

And have you forgotten the encouraging words God spoke to you as his children? He said, "My child, don't make light of the LORD's discipline, and don't give up when he corrects you. For the LORD disciplines those he loves, and he punishes each one he accepts as his child." As you endure this divine discipline, remember that God is treating you as his own children. Who ever heard of a child who is never disciplined by its father? If God doesn't discipline you as he does all of his children, it means that you are illegitimate and are not really his children at all. Since we respected our earthly fathers who disciplined us, shouldn't we submit even more to the discipline of the Father of our spirits, and live forever? For our earthly fathers disciplined us for a few years, doing the best they knew how. But God's discipline is always good for us, so that we might share in his holiness. No discipline is enjoyable while it is happening—it's painful! But afterward there will be a peaceful harvest of right living for those who are trained in this way (Heb. 12:5–11 NLT).

The writer of Hebrews teaches us that when we were disciplined by our earthly fathers, we respected them. That is the basis for the fear of the Lord—respect. And here is the paradox of the fear of the Lord: It produces a *peaceful* harvest of right living. It is the only type of fear that produces *peace*.

In a previous chapter, we talked about God's love casting out fear, because fear has to do with punishment (1 John 4:18). So is that a contradiction to the fear of the Lord? No. The fear of punishment talked about in 1 John is about condemnation and eternal punishment—hell. It is a tormenting fear that is not consistent with the love of God. Every person who has a personal relationship with Jesus Christ should have no fear of eternal condemnation (Rom. 8:1). God's unconditional, perfect love casts out all dread of condemnation and punishment from our God. We know and understand we are in his grace and mercy. His correction or punishment is only used for getting us on the right track, like any parent would do for his children.

Jesus, the Perfect Picture of God

Throughout the Old Testament, God would repeatedly try to correct and draw his rebellious children, the Israelites, back into a right relationship with him. He wanted to bless them. He wanted the whole world to see his glory and goodness through his people. He would repeatedly show them grace and mercy every time they came back to him. It was only when their rebellion went to extremes, such as worshipping other gods, killing their own children, and adopting the ungodly practices of the nations around them, that God would mete out severe punishment. God had established moral laws and a system of worship he wanted Israel to live by, and a sacrificial system for when they sinned. God made a distinction between willful sin and disobedience and the moral failures that happen as a result of people being imperfect. God was trying to display to the world what it meant to love God, live a holy life set apart for him, and understand that he forgives sin when a proper sacrifice is made and people repent.

Ultimately, what God was revealing in the Old Testament about who he is would be fully revealed in Jesus Christ in the New Testament.

> Long ago God spoke many times and in many ways to our ancestors through the prophets. And now in these final days, *he has spoken to us through his Son*. God promised everything to the Son as an inheritance, and through the Son he created the universe. The *Son radiates God's own glory and expresses the very character of God*, and he sustains everything by the mighty power of his command. When he had cleansed us from our sins, he sat down in the place of honor at the right hand of the majestic God in heaven (Heb. 1:1–4 NLT, emphasis mine).

Jesus would be the very expression of all that God is. So if we want to understand why we should fear God, we should learn about who he is through Jesus's life. Let's do a quick survey of the nature of Jesus:

1. He went around doing good and setting people free from demonic oppression.

"God anointed Jesus of Nazareth with the Holy Spirit and power, and how he went around doing good and healing all who were under the power of the devil, because God was with him" (Acts 10:38).

2. He responded to sinners with love and grace, not condemnation.

> The teachers of the law and the Pharisees brought in a woman caught in adultery. They made her stand before the group and said to Jesus, "Teacher, this woman was caught in the act of adultery. In

the Law Moses commanded us to stone such women. Now what do you say?"

They were using this question as a trap, in order to have a basis for accusing him. But Jesus bent down and started to write on the ground with his finger. When they kept on questioning him, he straightened up and said to them, "If any one of you is without sin, let him be the first to throw a stone at her." Again he stooped down and wrote on the ground.

At this, those who heard began to go away one at a time, the older ones first, until only Jesus was left, with the woman still standing there. Jesus straightened up and asked her, "Woman, where are they? Has no one condemned you?"

"No one, sir," she said.

"Then neither do I condemn you," Jesus declared. "Go now and leave your life of sin." (John 8:3–11)

3. Jesus came to give up his life to forgive and save the world.

"For God did not send his Son into the world to condemn the world, but to save the world through him" (John 3:17).

4. Jesus was filled with compassion

"When Jesus landed and saw a large crowd, he had compassion on them and healed their sick," (Matt. 14:14).

"When he saw the crowds, he had compassion on them, because they were harassed and helpless" (Matt. 9:36).

"Jesus called his disciples to him and said, 'I have compassion for these people; they have already been with me three days and have nothing to eat. I do not want to send them away hungry, or they may collapse on the way'" (Matt. 15:32).

"A man with leprosy came to him and begged him on his knees, 'If you are willing, you can make me clean.' Filled with compassion, Jesus reached out his hand and touched the man.

"'I am willing,' he said. 'Be clean!' Immediately the leprosy left him and he was cured" (Mark 1:40–42).

5. Jesus's correction of His followers produced maturity.

Clearly, Jesus had many opportunities to correct his closest followers. Peter's impulsivity, Thomas's doubting, the disciples' "little faith," and even their nap-taking in the Garden of Gethsemane. Jesus's rebuke and correction in each case was meant to produce righteousness and spiritual maturity. None of it was done in a way that condemned and made the disciples terrified of Jesus. In fact, the opposite happened. Their loyalty and commitment grew to the point that almost every one of them would give his life for Christ. Jesus, as the exact representation of God, didn't display the hellfire-and-brimstone God that some would believe he is. He confirmed the truths of the Old Testament: that God is a God of compassion, rich in mercy and slow to anger. But he is also a fair God who won't let the unjust go unpunished. The people Jesus got really angry at were the religious hypocrites who were filled with corrupt motives and were in direct opposition and rebellion to Christ.

True religion is marked by a reverent regard for God, an awe of his power and majesty, a dread of his punishment for those who rebel against him, and a deep revelation of his love for us.

Jerry Bridges, in his book *The Joy of Fearing God*, describes the healthy tension between loving and fearing God:

> In the physical realm there are two opposing forces called "centrifugal" and "centripetal." Centrifugal force tends to pull away from a center of rotation, while centripetal force pulls toward the center. A stone whirled about on the end of a string exerts centrifugal force on the string, while the string exerts centripetal force on the stone. Take away one and the other immediately disappears.
>
> These two opposing forces can help us understand something of the fear of God. The centrifugal force represents the attributes of God such as his holiness and sovereignty that cause us to bow in awe and self-abasement before him. They hold us reverently distant from the one who, by the simple power of his word, created the universe out of nothing. The centripetal force represents the love of God. It surrounds us with grace and mercy and draws us with cords of love into the Father's warm embrace. To exercise a proper fear of God we must understand and respond to both these forces.[1]

The Fear of God Removes Other Fear

Another interesting paradox in the Bible is that the fear of God actually causes other fears to cease. We already addressed the idea that when God does correct us as a loving father does to his children, peace is produced because of right living. But the Bible also teaches that those who fear God and delight in living lives obedient to him are blessed and don't fear other things in life:

> Praise the LORD. Blessed is the man who fears the LORD, who finds great delight in his commands. His children will be mighty in the land; the generation of the upright will be blessed. Wealth and riches are in his house, and his righteousness endures forever.

Even in darkness light dawns for the upright, for the gracious and compassionate and righteous man. Good will come to him who is generous and lends freely, who conducts his affairs with justice. Surely he will never be shaken; a righteous man will be remembered forever. *He will have no fear of bad news*; his heart is steadfast, trusting in the LORD. *His heart is secure, he will have no fear*; in the end he will look in triumph on his foes (Ps. 112:1–8, emphasis mine).

God's favor and power are with those who fear him. If God is for you, who can be against you?

I read a quote not long ago from Pastor Al Martin that said, "The essential ingredients of the fear of God are correct concepts of the character of God, a pervasive sense of the presence of God and a constant awareness of our obligation to God."

Having a correct concept of God means that we understand his love, kindness, compassion, mercy, and all those attributes that help us to realize that a relationship with him is the greatest gift this life has to offer. It also means we understand he is holy, righteous, all-powerful, and just, and he is worthy of our deepest respect, admiration, and obedience. Knowing that he is ever-present means we have an assurance that he is always with us to help, love, encourage, and strengthen us. It also means that our relationship with God requires the greatest authenticity. All things are laid bare before him (Heb. 4:13). We've all heard the expression, "When the cat's away, the mice will play." Our God is never away. He knows us intimately. We will never be able to fool our God. There is no pretending. A true fear of God keeps us profoundly honest.

Finally, fear of God reminds us we have an obligation in this relationship. He must be number one in our lives over everything else. Nothing can be more important than him. He must be preeminent or Lord over our lives, which means our family, work, free time, possessions, and everything else about our lives come under his authority.

Fear the Lord so you can enjoy all the wonderful blessings and rewards God has for you. Fear him so you have nothing else to fear.

"Now all has been heard; here is the conclusion of the matter: Fear God and keep his commandments, for this is the whole [duty] of man" (Eccles. 12:13).

12

GET OFF THE GERBIL WHEEL

Recently I was having a conversation with a good friend over lunch. Before long, it moved into the topic of burnout. Not our own personal burnout, but the burnout of so many people around us. That's not to say we haven't had our share of conversations about fatigue and stress in our lives, but in that moment, the burnout we observed was about others around us, and many of them were Christians. Everywhere we turned, people were tapped out. Fried. Overwhelmed. As we analyzed why we thought this was happening, we came to the same conclusion: Many people are consumed with what the Bible calls "anxious striving." It's striving that never allows slowing down. It doesn't have room for rest or balance. It seems driven by some unknown, unidentified fear that believes that something bad will happen if one doesn't keep going.

Sometimes it's performance driven. Sometimes it's guilt driven. Often it's society driven. But in the end, it always produces anxiety. There is another subtle characteristic of this anxious striving—an inability to rest. It's as though somehow resting is bad—things won't get done, one can't be "lazy" (even though rest has nothing to do with laziness)—or perhaps an unrealized belief of one's inflated sense of importance. A person may feel that he is so critical to whatever pursuit, process, or outcome he is involved in that he is indispensible; he just can't stop to take a break. It's not necessarily ego (although in some cases it may be), just a false understanding of the bigger picture. Sometimes the striving comes from the fear that unless a person works harder than others, she may get passed up, overlooked, or penalized in some way. The striving occurs in just about any area: education, sports, job, or even relationships. It reminds me of a gerbil on a wheel. Running and running, expending much energy, but never getting anywhere.

Nowadays, parents feel a tremendous pressure to "develop" their children in many ways so they can be prepared and compete well in whatever arena they will face in the future. Kids are put in sports, art classes, music lessons, and karate lessons, sometimes all at the same time. A good friend of mine is a soccer coach and repeatedly watches her young ten-, eleven-, and twelve-year-old players come to practice early on a Saturday morning exhausted. After soccer, they will be whisked off to music lessons or dance class.

According to a CNN article:

Forty-one percent of 882 children ages 9–13 surveyed in a recent KidsHealth poll said they feel stressed either most of the time or always because they have too much to do. And more than three-quarters of those surveyed said that they wished they had more free time...Overscheduling is a growing problem for American families, according to Dr. Alvin Rosenfeld, author of *The Over-Scheduled Child: Avoiding the Hyper-Parenting Trap.*

"A cultural phenomenon is taking place where parents are being told that the right way to raise their kids is to involve them in every enrichment opportunity possible, even if it means leaving the entire family feeling anxious and stressed," he said.[1]

Look at the description of "anxious striving" in the book of Ecclesiastes and see if it sounds familiar: "What does a man get for all the toil and anxious striving with which he labors under the sun? All his days his work is pain and grief; even at night his mind does not rest. This too is meaningless" (Eccles. 2:22–23).

The Bible talks about a type of work or labor that is worrisome; it wears a person down repeatedly, rather than bringing a sense of accomplishment. The person isn't just tired from his work; he's stressed and anxious. And it never ceases. Solomon, in Ecclesiastes 2:23, says that even at night, the person's mind is not able to rest. How many people do you know who lie in bed at night unable to sleep because of minds that cannot rest? Thoughts of all that needs to be done, or thoughts of life's pressures, race mercilessly through their minds, not allowing the rest that is vital to their health.

Common Traits of Anxious Striving

Ironically, many pastors and others in vocational ministry seem to deal with this phenomenon of anxious striving in fairly high percentages. While I'm uncertain of the current percentage of people who burn out and resign from vocational ministry, the number is significant. On his blog, Thom S. Rainer talks about seven reasons pastors burn out. Rainer came up with the list based on hundreds of pastors he knew who had left the ministry because of burnout. Several of those reasons fit the characteristics of anxious striving.[2]

1. The 24-7 Mentality

The first on his list is the 24-7 mentality. Many pastors never turn off work in their minds. They never relax, always anticipating the next phone call or crisis. Certainly the 24-7 mindset is part of the anxious striving that anyone can fall prey to. Part of this mentality may exist because of the belief that rest is unnecessary, as we talked about previously. I will talk about the importance of rest shortly. God designed rest for his people. Even Jesus didn't go 24-7.

2. Pressure to Meet Everyone's Expectations

Another trait on Rainer's list is the idea of needing to meet everyone's expectations, even when one knows deep down it's not possible. I've talked about people-pleasing in another chapter, but it's worth addressing again. It's unrealistic and certainly unproductive to live life believing it is important or possible to meet everyone's expectations. It is a sure path to anxiety and burnout. We must learn to live with the fact that not everyone is going to be happy with us all the time. Some people may not like us. That's OK. Our identity doesn't come from others' opinions of us; it comes from the God who created us. Our worth and value comes from him, not from the approval of others. God has said in his word that our focus should be to please him, not man. Now that doesn't mean we don't have to live up to any expectations. There are reasonable expectations that we all must strive to meet because it's part of living life. But constant anxious striving to please everyone is useless.

3. Unwillingness to Let Go

Next is an unwillingness to let go. Rainer tells of a story of a pastor who was rushing to get to a meeting but felt compelled to quickly try to sort through all the new mail that had arrived. When Rainer asked him why he didn't have someone else do that for him, he had no answer, just a blank stare. The pastor quit the ministry three months later. The need to control everything is often rooted in insecurity and fear. *If I don't do it, who will? If it doesn't get done or I don't control the outcome, something bad will happen.* Now there may be some times where that is true, but for the person who can never let go, there are many times that it is not true. This is the false belief that a person is indispensible. Some people try to make themselves indispensible so that they can meet their need to feel important. Your life is important by virtue of God designing you, making you a unique masterpiece and giving you your own special purpose and good works to fulfill while you're here on planet earth. You don't have to strive to make yourself important.

4. Feeling the Need to Do Things One is Not Suited For

Another trait is trying to do tasks one is not suited for. It's the pressure to do everything well. So many people feel pressure to do things they are not good at. It can be a result of trying to meet other's expectations, or it can be a fear of failure, rooted in perfectionism. Some people try to fit molds that society or certain cultures deem important or valuable. In church settings, people often value or esteem speaking gifts over other gifts. Some folks who may be very strong in other areas may feel insecure or not valued if they aren't a part of a ministry that involves speaking or teaching. Whatever the reason, God wants us to be confident in who we are and comfortable with our strengths and our weaknesses.

Getting off the Gerbil Wheel

So how do we get off the gerbil wheel?

First of all, learn what God's priorities are for your life. There's a verse in the Bible familiar to many Christians, which I want to use as our starting point for learning how to stop our anxious striving: "Be still, and know that I am God" (Ps. 46:10).

What you may not know is that the Hebrew word that is translated "be still" also means "slacken." To slacken means to relax, loosen up, or slow down. When a person slackens his grip, he relaxes it or loosens it up. When a runner slackens his pace, he slows down. Get the picture?

The New American Standard translation of the Bible translates this verse as "Cease striving and know that I am God" (Ps. 46:10, NASB).

There's actually a verse in the Bible that tells us to relax, to slow down. But that's not all the verse is teaching us to do. It's not implying a perpetual vacation. There is the all-important word "and" that tells us there's something else God wants us to do besides cease striving. He says we should "know that I am God."

Once again the Hebrew word translated as "know" implies a knowledge that comes by careful observation that produces recognition and comprehension. In other words, God wants us to cease our frenzied, anxious striving in life, slow down, and take time to be in his presence, to observe who he is and receive revelation that helps us comprehend that idea that he is God. To know that he is God means we also know who he is and what *makes* him God.

The writer of the Psalm wrote about knowing this God while being surrounded with people who would worship wood and stone idols, the sun, moon, and stars, and many other worthless "gods."

Only One Thing

Many people throughout the Bible had significant changes in their perspectives when they got a better revelation of who God is. It changed the course of their lives. It changed their priorities. It changed their values. It put things in balance. Balance comes by spending time with God and figuring out what really matters.

There's an example of this in Luke 10:38–42:

As Jesus and his disciples were on their way, he came to a village where a woman named Martha opened her home to him. She had a sister called Mary, who sat at the Lord's feet listening to what he said. But Martha was distracted by all the preparations that had to be made. She came to him and asked, "Lord, don't you care that my sister has left me to do the work by myself? Tell her to help me!"

"Martha, Martha," the Lord answered, "you are worried and upset about many things, but *only one thing* is needed. Mary has chosen what is better, and it will not be taken away from her" (Luke 10:38–42, emphasis mine).

Jesus gives us a very accurate picture of what anxious striving looks like with Martha. She was distracted by things in life that were really not what mattered most. She had an opportunity to listen to words of life. She had the opportunity to sit in the presence of the Messiah, her Savior, and learn from him. But anxious striving caused her to be distracted by things that really didn't matter all that much. Her priorities were out of alignment, but she couldn't see it. In fact, she felt her sister should be doing the same thing she was. Jesus points out that this is not just about Martha's distraction of preparing for her house guests. He tells her that there are many things that are worrying her and making her upset. She's living in a state of worry. His answer for her? "Only one thing." Spend time with him like Mary was. Make *being* with Jesus a priority over just *doing* for him.

It's amazing how many Christians are so busy, so distracted, so worried and upset, right in the middle of *doing* things for Christ. Perhaps you need to step off the gerbil wheel and sit down in God's presence. Quiet yourself. Sit at Jesus's feet and begin to listen to what he says. Ask *him* what he expects of you. Ask him what he *doesn't* expect of you. You might be surprised at his answer.

Jesus wants us to have plenty of time with him, learning from him so we know what really matters in life, to know what to spend our time on, to know what to believe about ourselves and others. When we get some perspective about who our God is, we realize we don't need to be worried and upset about so many things.

One of my favorite Psalms about perspective is written by Asaph. Asaph experienced something that perhaps many of us feel from time to time: that the bad guys always seem to get ahead. Asaph is feeling pretty discouraged about trying to live a righteous life. It seems all around him wicked people are prospering, and they don't seem to have struggles or burdens. They seem to get away with their evil behavior. But *only one thing* is needed for Asaph, just like what was needed for Martha: He needed to get into God's presence.

> Surely God is good to Israel, to those who are pure in heart. But as for me, my feet had almost slipped; I had nearly lost my foothold. For I envied the arrogant when I saw the prosperity of the wicked. They have no struggles; their bodies are healthy and strong. They are free from the burdens common to man; they are not plagued by human ills. Therefore pride is their necklace; they clothe themselves with violence. From their callous hearts comes iniquity; the evil conceits of their minds know no limits. They scoff, and speak with malice; in their arrogance they threaten oppression...
>
> This is what the wicked are like—always carefree, they increase in wealth. Surely in vain have I kept my heart pure; in vain have I washed my hands in innocence. All day long I have been plagued; I have been punished every morning. If I had said, "I will speak thus," I would have betrayed your children. When I tried to understand all this, it was oppressive to me till I entered the sanctuary of God; then I understood their final destiny. Surely you place them on slippery ground; you cast them down to ruin...
>
> When my heart was grieved and my spirit embittered, I was senseless and ignorant; I was a brute beast before you. Yet I am always with you; you hold me by my right hand. You guide me with your counsel, and afterward you will take me into glory. Whom have I in heaven but you? And earth has nothing I desire besides you. My flesh and my heart may fail, but God is the strength of

my heart and my portion forever. Those who are far from you will perish; you destroy all who are unfaithful to you. But as for me, it is good to be near God. I have made the Sovereign LORD my refuge; I will tell of all your deeds (Ps. 73:1–8, 12–18, 21–28).

Asaph says that once he entered the sanctuary of God, symbolic for the intimate presence of God, he finally understood the truth. His perspective came back. He realized, with God's help, that evil people are on slippery ground. There is justice awaiting them. Not only that, Asaph also realizes that the Lord is always with him, guiding him and giving him the hope of a wonderful future. Asaph's righteous living is not in vain. He remembers that God is his constant source of strength and blessing forever. Being near to God is the best place he can be. Asaph stills himself, slows down, relaxes in the presence of God, and once again knows his God.

The Perfect Example

Of course the most perfect example of one who didn't live on the gerbil wheel is Jesus himself: "But Jesus often withdrew to lonely places and prayed" (Luke 5:16).

Even Jesus himself knew the importance of getting away to some place quiet and spending time in his Father's presence. If it was necessary for Jesus, it's necessary for us. Jesus even told his disciples that they needed to get away to a quiet place and rest. He said, "Come with me…to a quiet place" in Mark 6:

The apostles gathered around Jesus and reported to him all they had done and taught. Then, because so many people were coming and going that they did not even have a chance to eat, he said to them, "Come with me by yourselves to a quiet place and get some rest." So they went away by themselves in a boat to a solitary place (Mark 6:30–33).

Jesus's disciples were very busy working and ministering. In fact, they were so busy, they couldn't even find time to eat. Jesus, knowing the importance of rest and balance, tells them to come with him to a quiet place. He wasn't the CEO who told his employees to take some time off as he sat in his office burning the midnight oil. He was going to the quiet place himself to get some rest.

The Giver of Rest

The Bible describes Jesus as the giver of rest in Matthew 11: "Come to me, all you who are weary and burdened, and I will give you rest. Take my yoke upon you and learn from me, for I am gentle and humble in heart, and you will find rest for your souls. For my yoke is easy and my burden is light" (Matt. 11:28–30).

Jesus is the New Testament version of Sabbath. God had instituted (and commanded) that his people would remember the Sabbath and keep it holy. They were to take time off and rest on the day the Lord declared as Sabbath. To not honor the Sabbath was to sin. God even designated that the land would get its own Sabbath, knowing that all those things that "rest" will be more productive in the long run. Giving the land a chance to rest from having crops planted in it would yield bigger and better harvests in the future. People who are rested and balanced in life are more productive. People who are burned out produce relatively little. God understood all that.

When Jesus gave people rest, it wasn't just that he had them sit down or take a nap. He unburdened them. He unburdened them from their sins by forgiving them. He gave those he forgave a new yoke that is easy to bear. He gives rest for our very souls.

Jesus would also unburden people physically by healing them.

That's why Jesus healed on the Sabbath—he was unburdening people, lightening their load in life, and giving them some rest from physical affliction. The Pharisees didn't understand because of their legalism and hatred of Jesus. Jesus explained to them that he was Lord of the Sabbath.

"For the Son of Man is Lord of the Sabbath" (Matt. 12:4).

In other words, he literally ruled over and personified Sabbath rest. Get off the gerbil wheel. Learn from the one who is your Sabbath and find rest for your soul.

13

IT'S TIME TO DREAM!

I've never been much of a dreamer. In fact, I would say I'm a bit of pragmatist (not that dreamers can't be pragmatic!). Lots of decisions I make about my life tend to be determined by whatever I consider to be the practical or logical thing to do. When I graduated from high school, I never had big dreams about what I wanted to do with my life. My whole thought process regarding my future was as follows: I need to get a job that pays more than waiting tables in Billy Bob's burger joint, so I better get a college degree in a high-paying field.

When I was a senior in high school, my math instructor was talking to our class about career options for those who were strong in math. He mentioned some well-paying fields, and one in particular stuck out to me: computers. I asked him about the various types of jobs within the field and as he described several options, I landed on computer programmer. It was the early 1980s, and working with computers and developing software wasn't as prevalent in high school then as it is today. All I knew from what my instructor had explained was that it paid well, and I had to be able to think logically and analytically. For my pragmatic self, that was all I needed to know. I knew I was analytical, and I wanted to earn good money. So, off

I went to college to get my bachelor's degree in computer science, knowing very little about the field and having no great aspirations to become a software developer. I graduated four years later with my degree and spent the next twelve years doing analysis and design of computer software. Did I love it? Not really. I enjoyed it some days and was pretty good at it. But it wasn't my dream career. It was just practical: good salary, medical benefits, and paid vacation. While it served a purpose for which I have always been thankful (including meeting another programmer who became my wonderful husband), God had something more for my life than just a good job for paying the bills.

Moving from Fear to Faith

During my first year of college, my life took a radical turn because of my decision to commit my life to Jesus Christ. During those early years, God began healing hurts and teaching me new ways of thinking and looking at life. He also challenged me to try new things, like teaching kids' Sunday school classes and leading adult Bible studies. As I shared earlier in the book, my initial response was complete and utter fear of being in front of people. But as I stepped out anyway and tried, I also began to discover people were really helped by my teaching. God used me to be a catalyst of change in their lives. Soon people would come to me for counseling. God began expanding my horizons, getting me out of my somewhat small comfort zone.

And something amazing happened. I found there were things that I loved to do, and I began to dream about new possibilities for the future. Moving from fear to faith will do that for you. Faith opens the door for things that used to seem impossible or unimaginable, because faith means trusting a God who loves you, knows your gifting, abilities, and the desires of your heart, and can do supernatural things to help you realize your full potential. That's why Jesus said he came to give us life, and give it more abundantly.

"The thief does not come except to steal, and to kill, and to destroy. I have come that they may have life, and that they may have it more abundantly" (John 10:10 NKJV).

One Bible translation says that he came to give us life to the full. That doesn't mean life is full because you have twenty-seven appointments crammed into your schedule this week. It means you can have a life that is rewarding and fulfilling, not empty and meaningless. It means experiencing your full potential. Jesus says that your spiritual enemy, Satan, wants to steal, kill, and destroy your life. If not physically, then he wants to do it emotionally, mentally, and spiritually by causing you to believe things that are not true and that ultimately cause you pain and fear. Satan is called the Father of Lies. He wants to destroy you with lies. Jesus said that when you know the truth, God's truth about who you really are and who he really is, that truth will set you free (John 8:32).

At about the twelve-year mark of working in the computer field, I began getting restless and feeling unfulfilled in what I was doing. My true love was helping people heal and grow personally and spiritually. One day, God spoke to me about getting my degree in counseling. My first reaction was that of angst. I hadn't been in school in years, I had a full-time career, and it would be a dramatic life change. But I was at a point in my faith at which I was ready to trust God and take this huge step. I had just put my application in the mail for graduate school, and I found out I was pregnant. It was not planned and immediately fear rose again, this time in the form of doubting I could go to graduate school and be a new mom at the same time. I was nervous just at the thought of being a new mom, and now I was going to try to do both things at once! For what seemed like the thousandth time in my life, I looked fear in the face and said, "I believe God is leading me. In faith, I'm going to do this."

Part of this new faith journey included resigning from my computer job and becoming a stay-at-home mom and student. Our income was cut in half, and our expenses increased as we now had a child and graduate school to pay for, but God repeatedly showed himself faithful in providing financially for us. Women from church would volunteer to help watch my son so I could study. By the time I had to do my internship, my son was entering school, which allowed for me to work while he was in school.

I got my master's degree and was going to prepare for licensing when God was going to challenge my faith yet again. It happened when I went away to a prayer cabin to spend a few days alone with the Lord. I try to get away once a year. It's my chance to seek God without distraction and give him my undivided attention. As I was at the prayer cabin, I was reading the following verses in Isaiah 54: "Enlarge the place of your tent, stretch your tent curtains wide, do not hold back; lengthen your cords, strengthen your stakes. For you will spread out to the right and to the left" (Isa. 54:2–3).

I was deeply moved when I read the verses. In fact, for no reason I could understand, tears began rolling down my cheeks. I knew God was speaking to me about them, but I wasn't sure what he was trying to tell me. It was obvious he wanted me to do something to prepare for more in my future. So I asked him what it was he wanted me to do, and I heard him speak clearly to my heart, "Get your ministry license."

My initial reaction was shock. "Wait a minute, God, I just finished graduate school to become a counselor. I'm going to work in a Christian counseling center. Why do I need a ministry license? Besides, I don't have the training for a ministry license, so I'd have to get more schooling. Did I hear you right?"

And God simply answered, "Yes. Get your ministry license. I'm preparing you for more."

In all honesty, the last thing I wanted to do was go back to school. And I had absolutely no idea how God was going to integrate my professional psychology training with a ministry license. Once again I felt anxiety, and once again I made up my mind that God is always right and I needed to trust him. So I began classes to get my ministry license. I finished in a couple of years, got my license, and said, "Now what, God?"

Very often the journey of faith is revealed only one step at a time. God doesn't show us everything at once, perhaps for good reason. Maybe we would get too freaked out if he did. I don't know. But one thing I do know is no matter what, he wants us to trust him and to get out of the boat. There's no other way to live a life of faith instead of fear than to listen to the voice of God that calls you out of your boat of safety, your comfort zone, and calls you to walk on the water with Jesus. It doesn't always make sense in your natural mind because you don't get to see the end result right away. But God knows where he's leading you.

Not long after getting my ministry license, I was asked to join our pastoral staff at my church as the adult discipleship and counseling pastor, the two things in my life that I was most passionate about. Helping people heal and grow spiritually and emotionally. Many things I had experienced in my life up to that point were woven into this new opportunity.

After three years in that staff position, God called me out of it to begin writing, first articles for a women's website, then this book. I also began a private counseling practice, which allowed me to broaden the scope of people I counseled beyond my own church. And doors opened to speak at women's events and retreats. God has planted dreams in me that would have been beyond my wildest imaginations just a few years ago. When we're able to let go of our fears and walk in faith and courage, God is able to do infinitely more in and through our lives than we ever thought possible.

"Now all glory to God, who is able, through his mighty power at work within us, to accomplish infinitely more than we might ask or think" (Eph. 3:20–21 NLT).

God can do more in and through you than you could ever even imagine.

Dreams Don't Always Come Easy

Joseph was a young man of seventeen when God gave him an incredible dream. He would one day be the second in command of the most powerful nation in the world at that time, Egypt. Imagine God giving this kind dream to a seventeen-year-old. As any young man might, Joseph got a bit zealous in sharing his dream with his family. To complicate matters, part of the dream included Joseph's brothers and parents bowing to him, which Joseph was only too willing to share. Needless to say, it didn't go over well.

Genesis 37–50 contains the long, winding road to the fulfillment of the dream God gave Joseph. It began with his brothers selling him into slavery out of their anger and hatred toward him. The journey also included a fairly long stint in prison because of a false accusation. Yet in each situation, the Bible says God was with Joseph and gave him favor with those around him because of his integrity. There were many tests of Joseph's faith through the years between the time God gave him his dream and the time of its fulfillment. From the moment God told him he would become a powerful leader in Egypt, circumstances screamed differently. He became a slave, then a prisoner. At any point, Joseph, not understanding why these things were happening, could have given up on the dream and stopped believing God. But he didn't. What Joseph didn't realize was that God would use all of the difficulties to strengthen and mature Joseph. At seventeen, Joseph wasn't ready to assume one of the most powerful positions in the world. He didn't know that when he assumed that role, it would be in the midst of a famine that would jeopardize his family and his nation, Israel.

"He called for a famine on the land of Canaan, cutting off its food supply. Then he sent someone to Egypt ahead of them—Joseph, who was sold as a slave. They bruised his feet with fetters and placed his neck in an iron collar. Until the time came to fulfill his dreams, the LORD tested Joseph's character" (Ps. 105:16–19 NLT).

Sometimes the bigger the dreams, the bigger the tests. Sometimes what appears to be big problems and obstacles to our dreams are actually God's tools for shaping us and getting us ready. The bigger the dreams, the greater the need for character.

Often it is hard for us to see how God uses the things in our lives that have seemed unfair, difficult, and purposeless. But God promises that he will work all things together for our good if we let him.

"And we know that all things work together for good to those who love God, to those who are the called according to His purpose" (Rom. 8:27–29 NKJV).

Remember, Jesus warned his followers that in this world we would have trouble, but we should take heart because he would help us overcome. Not only that, he would take the troubles and work them for our good.

There is a young woman in our church who was diagnosed with cancer not long ago. Just hearing the word *cancer* can strike fear in the hearts of most people. In faith, she walked through the journey of surgeries, cancer treatments, and financial challenges. Like most of us, she experienced ups and downs, questions, and tests of her faith. She is now cancer-free and has a dream of being used by God to help other women who are facing the same thing she has faced. God is helping her take her worst nightmare and turn it into an avenue of hope and help for others. I remember the first time she was asked to speak to a group of women. The joy that radiated from her was beautiful. Only God in his amazing goodness can take even our darkest times and work good from them. He can create dreams out of difficult places.

Remember Mary in the first chapter? Recently I got the privilege of seeing one of her biggest dreams fulfilled. It has been her heart's desire to one day have retreats for women that would bring deep healing and intimacy with God. After seven years of praying for God to help this dream come to pass, she was able to have her first retreat. Every woman who attended the retreat shared how her life had been incredibly impacted by the truth and power of God. The testimonies were remarkable. God had taken the shambles of Mary's life, the intense fears, the tremendous brokenness, and through her faith not only healed and transformed her life, but now through her brought healing and transformation into the lives of other women.

This life will never be perfect: wars, violence, cancer, economic crisis, famine, natural disasters. Many things could keep our hearts gripped with fear. But God has called us out of fear into a life of faith and hope. Hope not only for this life, but for a life beyond this one. The good news is that this life is not the final destination in our journey. Jesus promised us that if we keep trusting him, we have something much, much better awaiting us. A place called heaven, the city of God where his Father's house is. And Jesus is preparing a place for you there right now.

"Do not let your hearts be troubled. Trust in God; trust also in me. In my Father's house are many rooms; if it were not so, I would have told you. I am going there to prepare a place for you. And if I go and prepare a place for you, I will come back and take you to be with me that you also may be where I am" (John 14:1–3).

The apostle John was given a beautiful vision of the place God has prepared for those who trust Him:

Then I saw a new heaven and a new earth, for the first heaven and the first earth had passed away, and there was no longer any sea. I saw the Holy City, the new Jerusalem, coming down out of heaven from God, prepared as a bride beautifully dressed for her husband. And I heard a loud voice from the throne saying, "Now the dwelling of God is with men, and he will live with them. They will be his people, and God himself will be with them and be their God.

He will wipe every tear from their eyes. There will be no more death or mourning or crying or pain, for the old order of things has passed away" (Rev. 21:1–4).

Can you imagine a place where there is no more death, crying, or pain—a place with nothing to fear?

If you've never started this journey from fear to faith, I invite you to do so now. There is a God who knows just where you are at. Your life matters to him. He loves you and has a wonderful plan for you, a plan to give you a more fulfilling life, no matter where you've come from or where you are at in life right now. It's never too late to start. He just asks one thing from you: that you would be willing to start a new life with him and let go of anything in your life that is wrong or sinful. The Bible says that we've all sinned and fallen short of God's glory. But God is ready to forgive us, make us clean in our hearts, and bring us into the loving relationship he has for us.

"Repent, then, and turn to God, so that your sins may be wiped out, that times of refreshing may come from the Lord, and that he may send the Christ, who has been appointed for you—even Jesus" (Acts 3:19–20).

"For the wages of sin is death, but the gift of God is eternal life in Christ Jesus our Lord" (Rom. 6:23).

God is ready and willing to give you the gift of real life, abundant and eternal. Not filled with fear, but filled with freedom and opportunities to realize your greatest potential.

Take the step of faith. It's time to stop letting fear hold you back.

14

ARE YOU AFRAID TO SUCCEED?

I'm sure you've heard the expression, "If at first you don't succeed, try, try again." Great advice, if in fact, you're willing to try again. However, if at first you don't succeed, perhaps it's because you're afraid to.

I was sitting with a client today when she made a statement that intrigued me. I made the comment that based on some feelings she had shared about her future, it almost seemed like she feared success. Her reaction was immediate, "Oh, I do! In fact I think I fear success more than I fear failure." She followed that statement with another: "I know so many people that are afraid of success!"

On the surface, that might appear to be an odd notion; however, research bears it out. Many people do fear success. Maybe you're one of them. We talk a lot about the fear of failure, but the fear of success is a bit like the other side of the same coin. In an article in *The Wall Street Journal*, Dr. Regina Dugan, former director of the Defense Advanced Research Projects Agency (DARPA), stated that "you can't lose your nerve for the big failure, because the nerve you need for the big success is the exact same nerve."[1]

Before I proceed further, I want to clarify what I mean by success. We are all familiar with the typical dictionary definition—getting or achieving wealth, respect, or fame. I'm not talking about those culturally defined forms of success. They may or may not be in line with God's plan for a person's life. I'm talking about the achievement of a personal goal, dream, or desire.

What Causes Fear of Success?

So what exactly causes people to be afraid of success?

1. The comfort zone. No matter how good success in an area of life may look to us, it would mean leaving the familiar, and frankly that has derailed many people. We like our comfort zones, even if they aren't comfortable! They should probably be called our *familiar* zones. We like to know what we've got. A job promotion may mean more work, leaving old work relationships behind, and many other things a person may feel uncomfortable about. There is the question of risk: *Do I dare risk giving up the known for the unknown?* This also could be thought of as the fear of change.

Going after a new achievement will likely require additional effort, commitment, and sacrifice. Sometimes coasting, while not glorious or glamorous, is easier than paying the price for success. Or at least on the surface it might seem easier. Let me give you an example: How many times have you encountered people who refuse to do the work of change in some area of their lives, for example, weight loss, battling an addiction, or freeing themselves from old, toxic thought patterns, and would rather stay in the status quo? Is the weight problem or addiction making their life better? No. Is it easier than change? Not necessarily. It's just familiar—and oddly more comfortable in their minds than working hard to change and be successful.

2. Feeling unworthy of success. Sometimes the fear of success takes the form of self-doubt, the feeling that you can't handle success. Perhaps it comes from messages from the past: "You'll never amount to anything," or "You just have to accept the fact that you'll never be good at _____." Or the self-doubt may have been planted in the mind of a person through constant comparisons to others: "I could never do what they do. I just don't have what it takes." Whatever the beliefs, fear of success can be closely tied to insecurity and feelings of inadequacy. Success is about much more than being talented. It's more often about hard work, perseverance, and the willingness to keep trying after failure.

Perhaps you've heard the quote, "Hard work beats talent when talent doesn't work hard." Talent can certainly help a person become successful, but it is not the only thing. In fact, the most accomplished people in any field, whether that field is athletic, artistic, or intellectual in nature, always comes at the cost of more hours of practice or work than others are willing to put in. The "greats" become great because they work harder than their peers.

Vince Lombardi has been considered by many people to be one of the best coaches in NFL history. Lombardi took his first job as head coach with the Green Bay Packers in 1959. The Packers were just coming off their worst season ever with a record of 1-10-1. Interestingly, it wasn't for lack of talent that their record was so bad. They had five future Hall of Famers on the team at the time. Lombardi implemented intense training and demanded total commitment from the players. In his career with the Packers, Lombardi would never have a losing season. He led the Packers to three consecutive NFL championships and two Super Bowl wins. In one of his many famous quotes, he said, "The price of success is hard work, dedication to the job at hand, determination that whether we win or lose, we have applied the best of ourselves to the task at hand."

Feeling unworthy of success can also stem from the inability to handle failure. Those who succeed know that failure is part of the process of success. Michael Jordan, one of the greatest basketball players of all time, said, "I have failed over and over in my life. That is why I succeed." Bill Cosby once said, "In order to succeed, your desire for success has to be greater than your fear of failure."

3. Fearing problems that come with success. We've all probably heard of the company manager who, after being promoted, ended up snubbed by former coworkers. Or what about those who become wealthy through business success? How often we hear stories of people coming out of the woodwork wanting money. Then there is the pressure of sustaining the wealth, the risks of investing, and new social pressures. When one achieves a personal success, jealous backlash can come from people who were once trusted. I have heard more than one story of a person who lost weight, successfully reaching a personal goal, only to have friends and loved ones criticize and attempt to derail that person's accomplishment.

Sabotaging the Future

A common attribute among those who fear success is that they become saboteurs of their own future. In an article in *Fortune* magazine, a CEO in a financial firm in Illinois tells of a young banker who, after his promotion to president of a division, began an affair with a coworker and eventually knocked her down the stairs. He lost a solid marriage and his career.[2] Maybe you are one who sabotages your own success. It doesn't have to be as dramatic as the banker. It could show up as chronic procrastination. Or constant starts and stops. Or maybe it's excuse making. Perhaps you're just not bringing your A-game to whatever situation you're trying to succeed at, and you know it.

Fear of success is often revealed in long patterns of underachievement by people who are capable of much more. They avoid setting goals for themselves, keeping the bar low.

According to a therapist in Philadelphia who works regularly with success-fearing executives, some people will actually begin to believe that they have a serious illness, oftentimes cancer, just as they are about to move up significantly in their careers.[3]

Before we get into some practical ways to combat the fear of success, I'd like to address what the Bible has to say on the topic.

What Does God Think about Success?

Does God care if you're successful, and if so, how does he define success?

In a previous chapter, I talked about a young man named Joseph, who at the age of seventeen was given a powerful dream from God. God showed him that one day his whole family would bow down to him. He would be in a tremendous position of power and authority. His brothers were angry and jealous of him, so they sold him into slavery, which began a course of hardship and testing in Joseph's life that would ultimately develop the character and faith in him that would be required for his future position of power. Early on in Joseph's journey, we learn something about the way God defines success and prosperity. Look at Genesis 39:2–6:

> *The* LORD *was with Joseph and he prospered*, and he lived in the house of his Egyptian master. When *his master saw that the* LORD *was with him and that the* LORD *gave him success* in everything he did, Joseph found favor in his eyes and became his attendant. Potiphar put him in charge of his household, and he entrusted to his care everything he owned. From the time he put him in charge of his household and of all that he owned, the LORD blessed the household of the Egyptian because of Joseph. The blessing of the LORD was on everything Potiphar had, both in the house and in the field. So he left in Joseph's care everything he had; with Joseph in charge, he did not concern himself with anything except the food he ate (Gen. 39:2–6, emphasis mine).

Notice that it says that the Lord was with Joseph and was *the source* of his success! The word in the original Hebrew languages that is translated as "prospered" in verse 2 is the same word that is translated as "success" in verse 3. How was Joseph successful or prosperous? He did well with whatever responsibilities and tasks he was given. He was trustworthy. It was obvious to his master. Because Joseph was a man of character and integrity, God's hand was upon him, and he had favor. Those around him were blessed.

When we live a life of godly integrity, when we work hard and faithfully in whatever tasks are before us, God will give us success. Albert Einstein said, "Try not to become a man of success, but a man of value." Joseph was valuable to Potiphar and would one day be valuable to Egypt and save his own people from famine. God didn't define his success as a position of status and power. Joseph was a success and prospered when he was a slave in Egypt because he was a person of value to those around him.

The Bible says that David, another man after God's heart, had great success because the Lord was with Him: "Saul was afraid of David, because the LORD was with David but had left Saul. So he sent David away from him and gave him command over a thousand men, and David led the troops in their campaigns. *In everything he did he had great success, because the LORD was with him*" (1 Sam. 18:12–14, emphasis mine).

So what can we do to ensure that the Lord will be with us and give us success?

1. Regularly seek God for wisdom and direction in your life. Do what he tells you.

Uzziah was sixteen years old when he became king, and he reigned in Jerusalem fifty-two years. His mother's name was Jecoliah; she was from Jerusalem. He did what was right in the eyes of the LORD, just as his father Amaziah had done. *He sought God* during the days of Zechariah, who instructed him in the fear of God. *As long as he sought the* LORD, *God gave him success* (2 Chron. 26:3–5, emphasis mine).

Even at the young age of sixteen, Uzziah knew that he needed God's wisdom and understanding. God sees things that we don't see. His wisdom and ways are higher than our own, and he knows the right path for our success. God knew how to get Joseph to become the second most powerful man in the known world during that time, and the path to power was the very opposite most of us human beings would believe would ever work. God knew.

2. Be very diligent in living by the Word of God, the Bible. Don't compromise.

> Be strong and very courageous. Be careful to obey all the law my servant Moses gave you; *do not turn from it to the right or to the left, that you may be successful wherever you go.* Do not let this Book of the Law depart from your mouth; meditate on it day and night, so that you may *be careful to do everything written in it. Then you will be prosperous and successful* (Josh. 1:7–8, emphasis mine).

The word "success" used in Joshua 1:7–8 literally means acting out of wisdom and understanding. It implies that one has intelligence and prudence that makes one successful. And this wisdom and intelligence comes from knowing the Bible very well and being careful to apply its principles in every area of life. God honors those who honor him and his word.

3. Trust God. Have faith that he wants you to succeed and prosper.

"Hezekiah trusted in the LORD, the God of Israel. There was no one like him among all the kings of Judah, either before him or after him. He held fast to the LORD and did not cease to follow him; he kept the commands the LORD had given Moses. And the LORD was with him; he was successful in whatever he undertook" (2 Kings 18:5–7).

"[H]e who trusts in the LORD will prosper" (Prov. 28:25b).

"'For I know the plans I have for you,' declares the LORD, 'plans to prosper you and not to harm you, plans to give you hope and a future'" (Jer. 29:11).

Part of God's prosperity includes our well-being and peace. That is what God told his people in Jeremiah 29:11: His plans were good toward them. He cared about their well-being. His people had been very rebellious toward him and as a result experienced captivity in Babylon. They had forfeited the blessings God had promised them by being disobedient. Yet his heart continued to desire their blessing. He wanted his people to live in peace, not harm, so he reminded them of his plans for them. God has good plans for you—plans to make you prosperous and give you great success if you are willing to seek him continually and obey what he teaches.

We addressed earlier that one of the reasons people fear success is that they feel unworthy of it, oftentimes because of what they've been told or lies that they believe about themselves. If you are one of those people who regularly lives beneath your God-given potential, believe what God says about you, not what you may have been told by others. You are not unworthy of success if you choose to seek God and live for him faithfully. In fact, it is his plan to prosper you and give you success. He wants to be with you continually and grant you favor so that your life will be a blessing to all those around you, just like Joseph's.

Stop sabotaging your success. Live by God's principles and his promises. Know that God is for you, not against you. *You* need to be for you, not against you! Remember, there is grace for your failures. Just as Michael Jordan and many others have realized, failure is the teacher on the path to success. If at first you don't succeed, try, try again.

The great leader Winston Churchill once said, "Success is not final, failure is not fatal, it is the courage to continue that counts."

Lastly, if you fear success because you're afraid to get out of your comfort zone, remember that whatever lies in your future, if God's hand is leading you, will be good. Trust God with your future. Stop trying to control everything in your life. Faith requires risk and trust. If you know God's heart is only good toward you, you don't have to fear where he will lead you. Success and its changes don't have to cause you stress and anxiety. You will be able to handle it. God will not ask you to do anything you are not able to handle. He will make you ready, just like he did with Joseph.

Well Done, Faithful One

There are a lot of things in my life that I would like to be successful at. I want to be a good wife and mother. I want to be a successful Bible teacher, writer, and counselor. I'd like to know that I've helped lives change for the better. So how do I measure my success in any of these areas? I try to faithfully seek God and apply his biblical principles in my life, but I'm far from perfect. I've had many mistakes and failures along the way in all the areas I want to succeed in. So how should I measure success? A perfect marriage and a perfect child? Of course not. Does my teaching and writing need to reach a certain number of people? One thousand? Ten thousand? One hundred thousand? Oftentimes success in our culture is defined by measurable outcomes. A successful writer will sell a certain number of books. We've covered what the Bible teaches regarding how to be successful, but how does God measure success?

When I think about how to measure success in my life, I think of the parable Jesus told about three servants. All were given some responsibility by their master according to their unique abilities. No one was given more than he or she could handle. Their master set them up for success, not failure. He knew what they could accomplish as individuals and gave them an opportunity. Each would be required to give an account of what he or she had accomplished regarding the tasks he had given:

Again, the Kingdom of Heaven can be illustrated by the story of a man going on a long trip. He called together his servants and entrusted his money to them while he was gone. He gave five bags of silver to one, two bags of silver to another, and one bag of silver to the last—dividing it in proportion to their abilities. He then left on his trip.

The servant who received the five bags of silver began to invest the money and earned five more. The servant with two bags of silver also went to work and earned two more. But the servant who received the one bag of silver dug a hole in the ground and hid the master's money.

After a long time their master returned from his trip and called them to give an account of how they had used his money. The servant to whom he had entrusted the five bags of silver came forward with five more and said, "Master, you gave me five bags of silver to invest, and I have earned five more."

The master was full of praise. "Well done, my good and faithful servant. You have been faithful in handling this small amount, so now I will give you many more responsibilities. Let's celebrate together!"

The servant who had received the two bags of silver came forward and said, "Master, you gave me two bags of silver to invest, and I have earned two more."

The master said, "Well done, my good and faithful servant. You have been faithful in handling this small amount, so now I will give you many more responsibilities. Let's celebrate together!"

Then the servant with the one bag of silver came and said, "Master, I knew you were a harsh man, harvesting crops you didn't plant and gathering crops you didn't cultivate. I was afraid I would lose your money, so I hid it in the earth. Look, here is your money back."

But the master replied, "You wicked and lazy servant! If you knew I harvested crops I didn't plant and gathered crops I didn't cultivate, why didn't you deposit my money in the bank? At least I could have gotten some interest on it."

Then he ordered, "Take the money from this servant, and give it to the one with the ten bags of silver. To those who use well what they are given, even more will be given, and they will have an abundance. But from those who do nothing, even what little they have will be taken away. Now throw this useless servant into outer darkness, where there will be weeping and gnashing of teeth" (Matt. 25:14–30).

Note what Jesus teaches us about success in this parable. Success to Jesus is faithfulness and diligence to what he asks of his servants. He doesn't expect everyone to accomplish the exact same things. The servants were given different amounts of money to manage because they had different abilities. However, Jesus didn't think that the servant with the five bags of silver was any more successful than the servant with two bags of silver. They were considered equally successful.

His response to both of them is the same: "The master was full of praise. 'Well done, my good and faithful servant. You have been faithful in handling this small amount, so now I will give you many more responsibilities. Let's celebrate together!'"

Jesus determines success based on faithfulness to what he asks of us, not on our status, position, or power in society. He doesn't necessarily measure success by outcomes, because some outcomes are out of our control. We can work hard, do our best, be faithful to God, and not always obtain good results. Our children may choose a destructive path in life despite our best efforts to raise them well. There will be influences in their lives that are out of our control that may override the investment we made in them as parents.

Remember what the famous coach Vince Lombardi said? "The price of success is hard work, dedication to the job at hand, determination that whether we win or lose, we have applied the best of ourselves to the task at hand." Success isn't about winning or losing; it's about knowing we have applied the best of ourselves.

Second, if we measure our own success by what we see other people do, we will be living by a false standard. No one can define success in your life but God alone, because he is the only one who knows what he designed your life to be.

Be yourself and do your best with the tasks you've been given in life. If you fail, receive God's grace and pardon and keep trying. And remember, God is celebrating your faithfulness. He's celebrating *you*! You make him proud. Be confident in who you are. You're awesome. Your life matters. You're loved. People in this world need what you have to offer.

And remember, if you want to be a success in life, live to hear the words, "Well done, my good and faithful servant, you have been faithful…"

Chapter 1: Your Life Matters

1. Charles R. Swindoll, *The Tale of the Tardy Oxcart* (Nashville, TN: Word Publishing, 1998), 215.

2. John Ortberg, *If You Want to Walk on Water, You've Got to Get Out of the Boat* (Grand Rapids, MI: Zondervan, 2001), 101.

Chapter 2: Scared to Death

1. Coco Ballantyne, "Can a Person Be Scared to Death?" *Scientific American*, January 30, 2009, http://www.scientificamerican.com/article/scared-to-death-heart-attack/.

2. Melinda Beck, "Science Shows Even the Fit Can Be Scared to Death," *The Wall Street Journal*, October 22, 2012, http://www.wsj.com/articles/SB10001424052970203400604578072900187957988.

Chapter 6: Becoming Confident in Who You Are

1. Bill Hybels, *Descending into Greatness* (Grand Rapids, MI: Zondervan, 1993), 115–16.

2. R. J. Larson, *Prophet* (Bloomington, MN: Bethany House Publishers, 2012), 19–20.

3. Erwin Raphael McManus, *Seizing Your Divine Moment* (Nashville, TN: Thomas Nelson, 2002), 76–77.

4. Spiros Zodhiates, *Conquering the Fear of Death* (Chattanooga, TN: AMG Publishers, 1982), 532–33.

Chapter 7: From Chicken to Hero

1. Charles Spurgeon, *Evening by Evening*(Gainesville, FL: Bridge-Logos, 2005), 145.

Chapter 9: The First Step Is the Scariest

1. David Kinnaman, *Unchristian* (Grand Rapids, MI: Baker Books, 2008), 43.

2. Ibid., 47.

Chapter 10: Stop Fearing Fear

1. Franklin D. Roosevelt, "Inaugural Address, March 4, 1933," in *The Public Papers of Franklin D. Roosevelt, Volume Two: The Year of Crisis, 1933*, ed. Samuel Rosenman (New York: Random House, 1938), 11–16.

Chapter 11: What Exactly is the Fear of God

1. Jerry Bridges, *The Joy of Fearing God* (Colorado Springs, CO: WaterBrook Press, 1997), 98.

Chapter 12: Get Off the Gerbil Wheel

1. Lisa Porterfield, "Experts: Despite Their Energy, Kids Still at Risk of Burnout," CNN, last modified September 2, 2014, http://www.cnn.com/2006/EDUCATION/08/30/overscheduled.kids/.

2. "Seven Reasons Pastors Burn Out," Thom S. Rainer, last modified September 18, 2013, http://thomrainer.com/2013/09/28/seven-reasons-pastors-burn-out/.

Chapter 14: Are You Afraid to Succeed?

1. Walt Mossberg, "Defense on the Offense," *The Wall Street Journal*, June 6, 2011.

2. Anne B. Fisher, "Are You Afraid of Success?" *Fortune*, July 8, 1996, http://archive.fortune.com/magazines/fortune/fortune_archive/1996/07/08/214330/index.htm.

3. Ibid.

Heather Wochnick is a therapist working in private practice. She counsels individuals, couples, and families on a wide range of mental health issues, including anxiety, depression, and self-esteem—many of which are driven by seemingly irrational, but deeply rooted, fears.

In addition to her master's degree in counseling, Wochnick brings real-life Christian experience to her therapeutic approach. As a Bible teacher, speaker and former pastor, she has taught Christian living to people of all ages for thirty years.

Her debut book, *Quit Freaking Out!*, combines modern mental health therapy and faith-based counseling. Wochnick currently lives in Prior Lake, Minnesota, with her husband and son.

Made in the USA
Charleston, SC
21 August 2015